P9-DBK-963

SEP – 8 2014

INSIDE THE INDUSTRY
MEDICINE

BY RICHARD REECE

INSIDE THE INDUSTRY
MEDICINE

BY RICHARD REECE

Content Consultant
Angelica Ellman Christie, MEd, GCFI
Director, Health Careers Program
South Carolina Area Health Education Consortium

ABDO
Publishing Company

CREDITS

Published by ABDO Publishing Company, 8000 West 78th Street, Edina, Minnesota 55439. Copyright © 2011 by Abdo Consulting Group, Inc. International copyrights reserved in all countries. No part of this book may be reproduced in any form without written permission from the publisher. The Essential Library™ is a trademark and logo of ABDO Publishing Company.

Printed in the United States of America,
North Mankato, Minnesota
112010
012011

 THIS BOOK CONTAINS AT LEAST 10% RECYCLED MATERIALS.

Editor: Karen Latchana Kenney
Copy Editor: Amy E. Quale
Interior Design and Production: Emily Love
Cover Design: Emily Love

Library of Congress Cataloging-in-Publication Data
Reece, Richard.
 Medicine / By Richard Reece.
    p. cm. -- (Inside the industry)
 Includes bibliographical references.
 ISBN 978-1-61714-802-6
 1. Medical personnel--Vocational guidance--Juvenile literature. I. Title.
 R690.R435 2011
 610.69'6--dc22
                                   2010039491

TABLE OF CONTENTS

Some of your first encounters with medical professionals are visits with a pediatrician, which is a doctor specializing in the care of children and babies.

IS A JOB IN MEDICINE FOR YOU?

"The good physician treats the disease; the great physician treats the patient who has the disease."[1]
—*Sir William Osler, MD*

Does it make you feel better to help someone who is hurting? Are you interested in health and anatomy? If this sounds like you, then you've probably already wondered about a medical career.

Most of us first encounter the medical world as patients. In fact, you were probably a patient before you were born. Throughout your life, you've seen doctors, nurses, and other medical professionals in action. Everything from routine checkups, sports injuries, life-threatening illnesses, or trauma may have brought you in contact with a variety of specially trained people. Medical professionals all have the common goal to make you well.

A job in medicine can impact hundreds of lives each year—both patients and the family members and friends who love and care for those patients. People in the medical industry often possess good

WORLD'S HEALTHIEST COUNTRIES

In 2008, *Forbes* magazine named the world's healthiest nations. Countries ranked higher if they had clean, easily accessible drinking water and modern sanitation systems. Factors such as hunger, undernourishment, and infant mortality were important in the ranking, as was the presence of tuberculosis. The *Forbes* editors also examined the number of physicians available per 1,000 people and the life expectancy of a healthy man.

The 15 healthiest nations in the world:

1. Iceland
2. Sweden
3. Finland
4. Germany
5. Switzerland
6. Australia
7. Denmark
8. Canada
9. Austria
10. Netherlands
11. United States
12. Israel
13. Czech Republic
14. Spain
15. France[2]

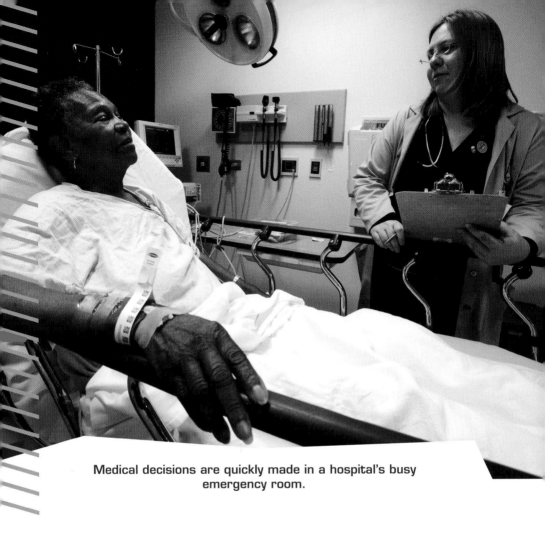

Medical decisions are quickly made in a hospital's busy emergency room.

communication skills and an aptitude for science. They are also lifelong learners, as the field of medicine is constantly changing due to new research. Often, doctors and other staff members must act as detectives, deciphering symptoms like clues and putting them together to identify a cause. Medical professionals must be committed, undergoing extensive and expensive training to meet the qualifications of their field. Once on the job, they may work long hours on behalf of the people they treat.

CHARACTERISTICS OF JOBS IN MEDICINE

Have you seen medical professionals, both fictional and real, on television? Screenwriters have long appreciated the real-life drama of this field. It's true that emergency room trauma surgeons make scores of split-second, life-or-death decisions in the course of their work. Other medical careers are much less dramatic, though just as necessary.

One of the most apparent qualities of the medical industry is its incredible variety. New specialties are constantly appearing as technical strides are made in medicine. Every specialty has its own educational and personal requirements and comes with a variety of earning potential. Today, medical care is a team effort. To be successful in a medical career, a medical professional needs to work closely and respectfully with patients as well as other professionals.

Jobs are booming in the medical industry, which is great news for someone interested

THE FATHER OF MEDICINE

Hippocrates, a Greek physician who lived from 460 to 377 BCE, is known as the father of medicine. Unlike many healers of his time, he based his medical practice on observation and the study of the human body. He held the belief that illness had a physical and rational explanation.

in a career in medicine. But do you wonder why jobs in medicine are increasing? Shouldn't medical advances result in more well people—and fewer people needed to care for the sick? There are several answers to those questions. The human population is increasing and people are living longer. That means they will encounter more naturally occurring health problems than earlier generations. Also, doctors make new discoveries about diseases and human ailments every day. These new discoveries drive new technologies, which then require new types of medical education. In 20 years, there will without a doubt be careers in medicine that do not exist today.

The possibility of new career specialties brings up another aspect of medical careers. In most cases, medical professionals do not simply go to school, learn skills, and keep repeating the same skills for their entire careers; as science and technology advance, medical personnel have to continue educating themselves. New procedures, new machines, and new challenges appear every year.

"We look for medicine to be an orderly field of knowledge and procedure. But it is not. It is an imperfect science, an enterprise of constantly changing knowledge, uncertain information, fallible individuals, and at the same time lives on the line. There is science in what we do, yes, but also habit, intuition, and sometimes plain old guessing. The gap between what we know and what we aim for persists. And this gap complicates everything we do."[3]

—Atul Gawande, MD

A SURVEY OF JOBS IN MEDICINE

When you think of medical professionals, doctors and nurses may come to mind. While these jobs are vital in medicine, they only scratch the surface of positions in this industry. There is a wide range of specialties, such as pathology, the study of diseases and their causes, and pediatrics, the care and treatment of children. There are even alternative practices such as acupuncture, where the practitioner inserts needles into various parts of the body to relieve pain or treat illness, and chiropractic, where the doctor adjusts the musculoskeletal system to relieve pain and promote general wellness. For every medical specialty, assistants and aides are needed to back up doctors and their staff. Pharmacy technicians, physical therapy assistants, and medical records technicians are just a few examples.

Public health professionals work to treat and prevent disease on a broad societal scale. They monitor epidemics and work to improve factors that influence health, such as public sanitation, personal hygiene, and immunizations. They may work in laboratories or in remote locations around the world. As the world becomes more developed, experts anticipate increasing concerns with new outbreaks of previously rare infectious illnesses.

New diseases may require new treatments and medicines, and there is currently a huge demand for those trained in biology and biotechnology to research and produce them. These professionals work in both public agencies and private companies.

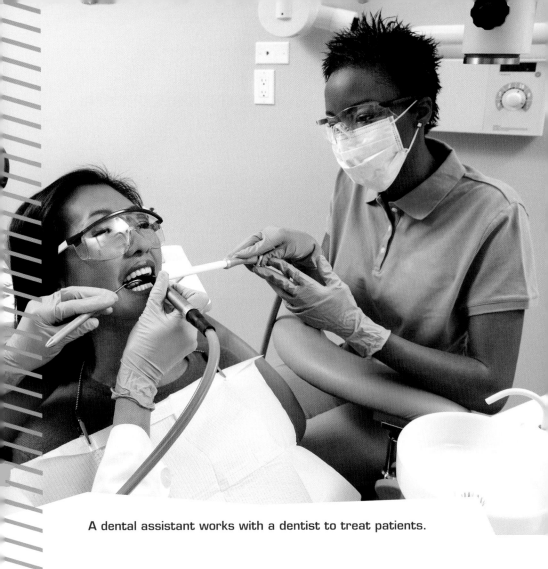

A dental assistant works with a dentist to treat patients.

While both professionals and patients tend to complain about the limitations and expense of medical insurance, the fact is that insurance is crucial in providing millions of people with the care they need. This industry needs creative thinkers who care for the people they serve and want to optimize efficiency while minimizing expense.

TEN POPULAR JOBS IN MEDICINE

This book will give you a look at the world of medical jobs. You'll also learn about four jobs in the field: physical therapist, pharmacist, neonatal nurse, and neurosurgeon. Discover what skills are needed for each job and what the journey looks like to enter these careers. Here are ten other popular professions in the medical industry, along with each job's main duties:

1. **Emergency medical technician (EMT) or paramedic:** Both EMTs and paramedics provide emergency medical care to victims before and during transportation to the hospital. They also assist other medical professionals in providing treatment.

2. **Pharmacy technician:** In a pharmacy, technicians prepare and dispense medications under the direct supervision of the pharmacist. They also provide customer service and perform administrative tasks.

3. **Home health aide:** A home health aide provides assistance and care to patients with illnesses or disabilities in their own homes.

4. **Medical secretary or transcriptionist:** These professionals prepare and maintain medical records and perform other administrative tasks.

5. **Dental assistant:** A dental assistant supports a dentist in carrying out clinical, laboratory, and

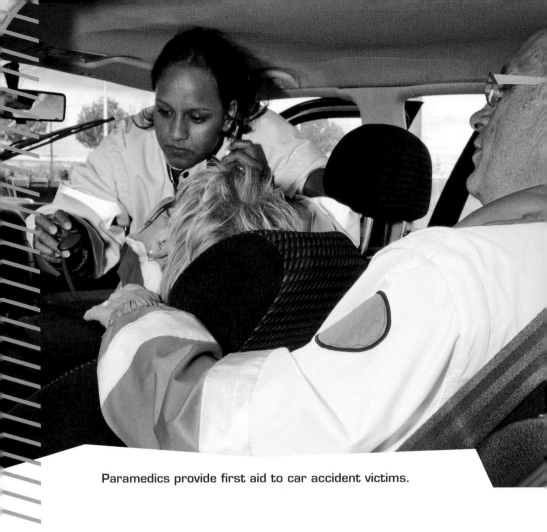

Paramedics provide first aid to car accident victims.

administrative duties, including sterilizing equipment
and taking X-rays.

6. **Advanced practice nurse or nurse practitioner:**
   With the oversight of a physician (onsite or through
   distance communication), these nurses diagnose
   and treat illness and disease and provide patient
   counseling and education.

7. **Health-care administrator:** A health-care administrator plans, coordinates, and supervises health-care facilities and their staffs.

8. **Nursing aide, orderly, or attendant:** These professionals work under the direct supervision of a nurse to perform a wide range of routine, nonmedical duties, such as moving patients.

9. **Mental health counselor:** A mental health counselor counsels families, individuals, groups, and couples to promote mental health and well-being.

10. **Medical records technician:** A medical records technician assembles and maintains patients' medical records to ensure quality, accuracy, accessibility, and security.

The most important factor in choosing any career is being able to honestly assess your own interests, skills, strengths, and challenges. If helping people is important to you, medicine can provide an incredibly fulfilling and continually evolving career.

A PRESIDENT WHO STUDIED MEDICINE

William Henry Harrison, the ninth US president, was the only president who studied to become a doctor. Apparently, the knowledge didn't help him. Harrison took his oath of office on March 4, 1841, which was an extremely cold day. He gave a 105-minute speech outdoors wearing neither a hat nor coat. He developed pneumonia and died in the White House exactly one month later.

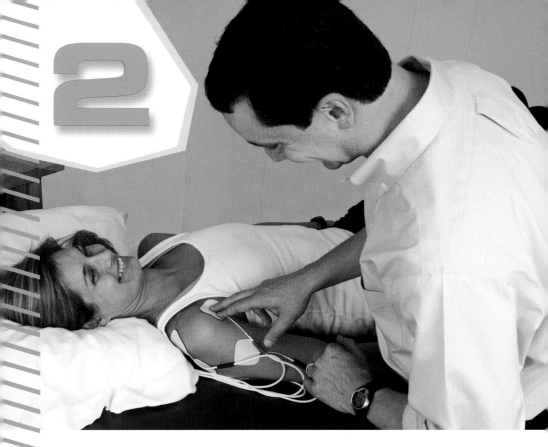

Electric stimulation is one tool physical therapists use
in treating patients.

WHAT IS A PHYSICAL
THERAPIST?

Did you know that by this time in your life, you
have almost certainly given or received physical
therapy? When you were a toddler and stubbed your toe,
what was the first thing your parent did? Your parent

probably held you until you stopped crying. When you had trouble going to sleep, maybe your parent gave you a gentle back rub to relax you. Today's professional physical therapists work with an impressive array of methods and technologies, but they have one thing in common—they all use human touch.

Modern physical therapists (also referred to as PTs) use heat and ice, water, electricity, massage, and various types of machines designed to assist in gaining flexibility or restoring strength to a given body part. Some treat all physical disabilities; others specialize in treating specific conditions such as arthritis, heart diseases, fractures, head injuries, and cerebral palsy. Many kinds of patients are treated with physical therapy. Some suffer from sports injuries. Others have been wounded in war. Many are victims of auto accidents or work injuries.

A physical therapist will first check a patient's medical history. Pain while walking, for instance, could be a result of anything from trauma or cancer to arthritis or a slipped spinal disk. Next, the physical therapist will try to measure the factors

AN ANCIENT ART

For thousands of years, people have recognized that warmth, sunlight, water, exercise, and massage are helpful in treating injuries. Just as professional sports teams today have trainers, the athletes and gladiators of ancient Greece and Rome turned to healers and even their fellow athletes when they broke bones, dislocated joints, or strained muscles.

A physical therapist's office is filled with different kinds of rehabilitation equipment.

involved in the patient's complaint: How much, exactly, is the patient's movement impaired? Are the patient's muscles weak or unresponsive? Finally, the physical therapist will estimate how much improvement the patient can expect and how long it will take for the patient to recover. The physical therapist works with both individual patients and groups. The therapist determines the treatment and sometimes (depending on the size of the staff) oversees an assistant in the facilitation of the treatment.

Some people have their sights set on a career in physical therapy during high school. Others may have encountered physical therapy when they participated in sports or exercised. However you decide to pursue this career, it is important to have respect for holistic wellness and a conviction that a person's body and mind work together to achieve a healthy balance.

WHAT IS A PHYSICAL THERAPIST'S WORK ENVIRONMENT?

Physical therapists work in an amazing variety of settings. Industrial clinics are places where they may treat workers' short-term injuries and teach them ways to prevent future injuries on the job. In schools, therapists treat children with disabilities. Therapists treat elderly patients in long-term care facilities. Community centers may sponsor programs that involve physical therapists, such as water aerobics for disabled adults. Mental health institutions employ physical therapists to help patients exercise and interact socially and to treat physical health problems specific to patients with disorders such as schizophrenia. The last few decades have seen an increase in clinics specializing in the treatment of sports injuries.

Physical therapists may also have independent practices. They might also consult with hospitals that are establishing physical therapy departments. Other physical therapists go into teaching physical therapy in universities or other training settings.

A physical therapist's office may look like any other medical office with a waiting room, clerical personnel, and magazines. Behind the scenes, though, you'll find a wide array of equipment including cold and warm water baths, exercise equipment, massage

IT'S THE LAW

The federally mandated Individuals with Disabilities Education Act (IDEA) requires that children with disabilities have access to services from physical therapists and other therapeutic and rehabilitative services. Under IDEA, infants and toddlers with disabilities and their families receive early intervention services. Children and youth receive special education and related services. The requirements of IDEA mean the demand for therapists in schools will continue to grow.

tables, infrared lamps, and ultrasound machines. A TENS machine (transcutaneous electrical nerve stimulation) beams an electric current through the skin and into injured areas to stop pain. Physical therapy departments in large hospitals have even more extensive layouts and may include swimming pools. These departments usually have teams of physical and occupational therapists who specialize in different treatments and disabilities. Patients such as stroke victims, amputees, or those with recent joint replacements may work with these teams.

Most full-time physical therapists work a 40-hour week, and some work evenings and weekends to fit their patients' schedules. Approximately 27 percent of physical therapists work part-time.[1]

HOW IS THE JOB MARKET FOR PHYSICAL THERAPISTS?

Physical therapists are in high demand. In 2008, there were approximately 185,500 physical therapists employed in the United States. They earned an average annual wage of $72,790, with the highest-paid 10 percent earning more than $104,350.[2]

The US Bureau of Labor Statistics expects employment of physical therapists to grow much faster than average—by 30 percent from 2008 to 2018. Job opportunities should continue to be good, especially in rural areas, because physical therapists tend to cluster in highly populated urban and suburban areas. Job opportunities should also be good in settings that treat elderly patients, such as orthopedics.[3]

There are several reasons for the expected increase in physical therapy positions. One is the increasing population

SATISFYING WORK

According to a 2007 survey conducted by the National Opinion Research Center at the University of Chicago, Illinois, 78.1 percent of physical therapists reported being "very satisfied" with their occupation.[4] In a similar survey by the *Wall Street Journal*'s CareerJournal.com, physical therapy was rated one of the eight most satisfying careers, based on intellectual stimulation, job security, having freedom and control in one's work, and personal contact with clients.[5]

of elderly, who are vulnerable to the kinds of conditions that require physical therapy. Also, people from the baby boomer generation—those born between 1946 and 1964—are currently at a high-risk age for heart attacks and strokes. Developments in medical technology and changes in what services insurance companies will pay for will also increase the need for physical therapists.

If medical care is getting better, why do we need more medical personnel? The need for physical therapists is a wonderful example. Medicine is saving more people every year, and as a result, more patients need rehabilitation. Physical therapy is a career with a great future, a very good salary, and a chance to change lives for the better.

A PROFILE OF A PHYSICAL THERAPIST

Dr. Steve Wynia is the director of a physical therapy clinic in Brooklyn Center, Minnesota. He became interested in physical therapy in high school, when he was injured and was treated by a physical therapist.

After high school, Wynia attended South Dakota State University and received his bachelor's degree in biological science. Before entering graduate school, Wynia volunteered at hospitals, nursing homes, and outpatient clinics.

Wynia then went on to the Mayo School of Health Sciences in Rochester, Minnesota, and received his master's degree in physical therapy. After working for a few years as a licensed physical therapist, he continued his education at the University of North Dakota to receive his PhD.

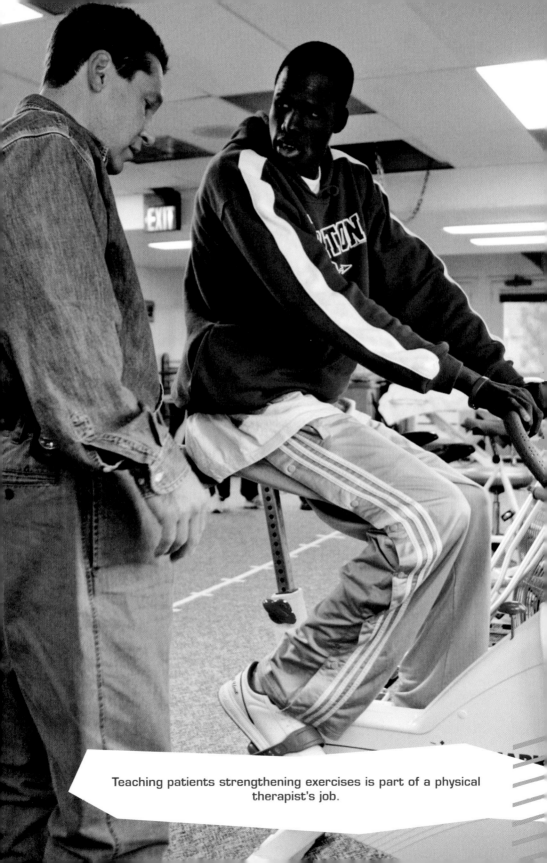

Teaching patients strengthening exercises is part of a physical therapist's job.

A typical five-day workweek for Wynia involves working eight hours a day seeing as many as 20 patients each day. His clinic has a variety of tools physical therapists can use on their patients, such as exercise machines, ultrasound machines, and electric stimulation devices. But, Wynia mostly likes to use his hands when treating patients.

Many physical therapists are satisfied with their jobs. Wynia agrees, saying that the best part is:

> Helping patients get back to a level of function that they were previously unable to achieve. Many times, patients come to our clinic and they are unable to work or sleep through the night or golf, and the treatment I provide is able to get them back to their normal routine.[6]

Some stressful parts of the job include dealing with insurance companies, including verifying patient benefits and securing reimbursements. Also, sometimes patients do not get better from their treatment. Patients count on physical therapists to help them recover so they can return to work. When this doesn't happen, it can be frustrating for both the physical therapist and the patient.

Wynia offers the following advice to students interested in a career in physical therapy:

> Learn about the profession. Call up a clinic and ask if you can shadow for a few hours. Most providers enjoy having students come in and watch. Shadow in multiple clinics. There are many specialties in physical therapy and a student may be drawn to one more than another. For example PTs can specialize in pediatrics, orthopedics, neurology, home

health, wound care, cardiac, in-patient hospital, etc. It's good to see a variety.[7]

A DAY IN THE LIFE OF A PHYSICAL THERAPIST

Physical therapists work in diverse settings, so a day in the life of one may be quite different from a day in the life of another. A typical day usually involves meeting patients, evaluating their progress, and directing them in the next steps in their respective treatments. Some of a therapist's time will involve hands-on treatment and some will consist of keeping up with paperwork.

Depending on the setting and a therapist's training, he or she may see patients with either a wide variety or a very specific set of needs. Some patients will be new and can require more time because they need to be evaluated, and a therapist will need to be caught up on their histories. Other patients are regulars who have already embarked on a treatment plan, and thus each appointment is more predictable.

A therapist assigns exercises to patients and tells them how important it is that they really do their exercises between sessions. Physical therapy patients usually are limited by their insurance to a certain number of sessions. For a therapist, patients who don't do their homework can be a source of frustration.

TOP FIVE QUESTIONS ABOUT BECOMING A PHYSICAL THERAPIST

1. *How long do I need to go to college?*
   Physical therapists need to have a bachelor's degree plus a master's or a doctoral degree, which typically requires six to seven years in college.

2. *What are the benefits of working as a physical therapist?*
   Physical therapists get to work closely with the people they treat. They help and encourage patients to recover a better quality of life. Patients come from all backgrounds, which allows physical therapists to meet many different kinds of people. Physical therapists' salaries and benefits are also excellent.

3. *What are the negative aspects of working as a physical therapist?*
   Patients do not always cooperate or follow their exercise regimens. For insurance reasons, physical therapists cannot always continue treatment as long as necessary for the best outcome. The insurance paperwork they have to complete can also be a headache.

4. *Are physical therapists satisfied with their jobs?*
   Yes! They have one of the highest job satisfaction ratings of any career. In a recent survey, they ranked second in job satisfaction of top occupations.[8]

5. *What qualities does a physical therapist absolutely require?*

   Physical therapists must be patient, be good teachers, and they need to love hands-on work with clients. Valuing personal wellness is also helpful for a physical therapist.

   It can be physically demanding to work as a physical therapist, so it is important to be physically fit and have the strength to work with patients.

   ## PHYSICAL THERAPY AIDES

   Physical therapy aides work under the close supervision of a physical therapist or a physical therapy assistant. Aides do routine tasks that involve preparing the patient and the treatment area. For instance, physical therapy aides keep the treatment area clean and well organized. They also help patients get to and from the treatment area. Employers usually require physical therapy aides to have a high school diploma. Most of an aide's training occurs on the job.

It takes physical strength to perform some therapeutic exercises on patients.

WOULD YOU MAKE A GOOD PHYSICAL THERAPIST?

f you are wondering, "Do I have the qualities it takes to succeed as a physical therapist?" you might want to break that question into two parts. First, ask yourself, "Do I have the qualities necessary to *enjoy* being a physical therapist?"

Then ask, "Do I have the skills that would help me to practice physical therapy?"

To enjoy a career as a physical therapist, you need to like people and want to help them. Often your patients will see their situations only in the short term—the pain or disability they feel at the moment. Part of your job will be to gain their trust as you partner with them on their journeys to better lives. When your compassion and confidence are genuine, your patients will feel it.

As far as skills go, this job requires some physical strength; mechanical aptitude, both as it applies to the body and to the equipment involved in treatment; observation; patience; and communication.

TROUBLE ROLLING OVER, BOY?

A dachshund had surgery for a back problem, but his recovery is going slowly. A cat landed on its feet but injured its hip. The old family dog is so sore with arthritis that it's difficult for her to go outside. Humans are not the only creatures who can benefit from physical therapy. This is why some veterinarians and veterinarian technicians have become certified in the rehabilitation of animals.

If you love animals, then helping four-legged friends with post-surgery recovery, arthritis, and chronic pain can be a satisfying career. The way to approach this goal is through a career path in veterinary science.

Animals can have injuries requiring specialized treatment plans. Animal physical therapists assist during surgery and recovery. They also help animals that have chronic pain and arthritis. The physical therapist's work speeds up healing time and helps animals during their recovery.

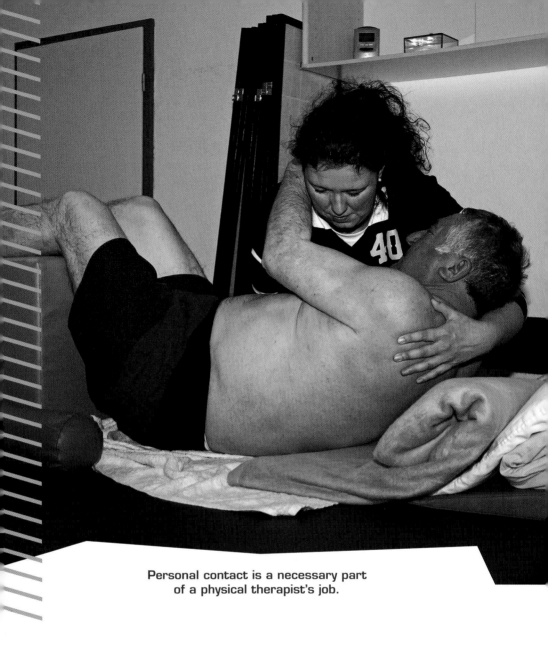

Personal contact is a necessary part
of a physical therapist's job.

HANDS-ON HEALING

Physical therapy may be the most hands-on branch of
medicine. It requires close bodily contact with people of all
ages and states of health. This can be challenging. A patient

in the course of treatment might vomit or lose bowel control, for example. A physical therapist deals with that while never forgetting the importance of treating his or her patient with dignity and empathy.

It's also important to have good emotional control. A physical therapist sometimes has to inflict pain on patients in order to make them better. A balance between your natural sympathy and your dedication to healing is something you will need every day on the job.

PATIENCE IS REQUIRED

Among the skills you will need to acquire as a physical therapist if you don't have them naturally, perhaps the most important

YOGA THERAPY

Yoga is a system of exercise, breathing, and meditation that originated in India. The practice is at least 5,000 years old, and it has always been used as a way to develop flexibility, strength, and balance. Although common in India, yoga therapy is an emerging field in the United States. Therapists adapt yoga poses to address muscular and skeletal problems.

In the United States, there is no system for licensing or accreditation of yoga therapists. Almost anyone trained in yoga and with some knowledge of anatomy, breathing, and meditation can become a yoga therapist. There are legitimate yoga therapists, however. Many have credentials in recognized medical fields such as physical therapy nursing.

is patience. Therapy, especially for serious injuries, can last months or even years. Patients can feel frustrated, but a physical therapist needs to be an example of patience during the recovery process.

ATHLETIC STRENGTH

The daily routine of a physical therapist requires endurance, stamina, and a wide range of motion. You may be kneeling, crouching, or demonstrating exercises, and you may also need to lift equipment and sometimes patients. Strong hands and arms are also important for massage or for repetitive manipulation of patients' limbs.

CAN YOU TEACH?

Physical therapists cannot always be with their patients. They need to teach patients and, most importantly, show them how to perform the activities that will improve their functioning. That way, patients can perform their exercises outside of therapy sessions. Physical therapists need to be able to communicate clearly on their patients' levels and notice whether patients are understanding.

SCIENCE AND TECHNOLOGICAL SKILLS

Much of the training you will need to become a physical therapist involves studying subjects such as biology, anatomy, and physiology. Computer literacy is also a huge help in the work of a physical therapist, both for record keeping and for keeping up with innovations in the field. And much of the work you will do will involve using machines or gadgets. If you are comfortable around or excited by mechanical tools, learning to be a physical therapist will be easier for you.

CHECKLIST

Is physical therapy right for you? Take a look at this checklist to see if this career is a good fit.

- *Do you take good care of your own physical fitness?*

- *Are you a good listener?*

- *Do you notice changes in people's appearance or mood?*

- *Can you explain things in a way people understand?*

- *Does helping people make you feel good?*

- *Are you okay having close physical contact with people?*

If most of your answers were yes, a career as a physical therapist could be in your future. If you answered no to more of the questions but still want to be a physical therapist, don't worry. If you don't have these qualities yet, hard work and determination can go a long way in helping you achieve your dream job.

HOW TO GET THERE

HIGH SCHOOL

In high school, get good grades in your classes and on standardized tests. Involve yourself in extracurricular activities that will show you are a well-rounded person. It is also important to know yourself. Evaluate your personal strengths, challenges, and the things that make you happy.

Ask questions about possible careers and institutions of higher learning, and research the answers—just as you're doing now.

If you are interested in becoming a physical therapist, pay special attention to your performance in science and math courses. You might also think about learning Spanish; the fastest growing population in the United States is Spanish speaking. Also, don't neglect English classes. They will improve your written and spoken communication skills.

Your physical fitness is also very important. Participate in school athletics. You don't have to make the varsity team to be in shape, though. Work on your endurance, strength, mobility, and balance. Those abilities will serve you well as a physical therapist; exercising, building strength, and learning to understand your body's capabilities are the very skills you will be teaching your clients.

Learn to pay attention to what you see. Notice the way people move and carry themselves. A person's gait and posture will tell you a lot about their mood or health. As a physical therapist, you'll become a trained expert in observing people this way. Why not start practicing?

VOLUNTEER EXPERIENCE

Admissions officers in physical therapy degree programs also look for volunteer experience from incoming students. Experience as a physical therapy aide, a history of leadership, and letters of recommendation from physical therapists or science teachers will help with college applications. Try to find a job, whether paid or volunteer, in a physical therapy clinic or a medical setting. It will not only give you a feel for the job, but it could result in gaining important contacts. If you can't actually find employment with a physical therapist, try job shadowing a physical therapist. Observing a physical therapist at work on a typical day and asking questions will give you valuable insight into this career.

COLLEGE AND BEYOND

Much of your undergraduate coursework will involve prerequisites, such as anatomy and physiology, chemistry, physics, statistics, psychology, and general biology. Be sure you know what undergraduate courses will be required by the graduate program you choose. Besides academic classes, much of your graduate coursework will involve actual clinical rotations. In these rotations, you will

"All schools require a certain number of observation hours of a PT. I highly, highly recommend you split them up between at least 3 different physical therapy places, preferably in different settings. Some schools might not care, but it will help a lot if you have a diverse experience before you come to school. Each PT and clinic is different and does things differently. There is no one way to do things. If you get all of your hours at one place, you might get that impression. Regarding different settings, observe in at least an outpatient orthopedic clinic and a hospital setting, maybe a nursing home too. This varied experience will mean a lot more to you in the end, believe me. Also, it will give you more options for getting letters of recommendation from a PT and open you up to the diversity of the field."[1]

—*Bridget Grace Regan, doctoral graduate student at Emory University*

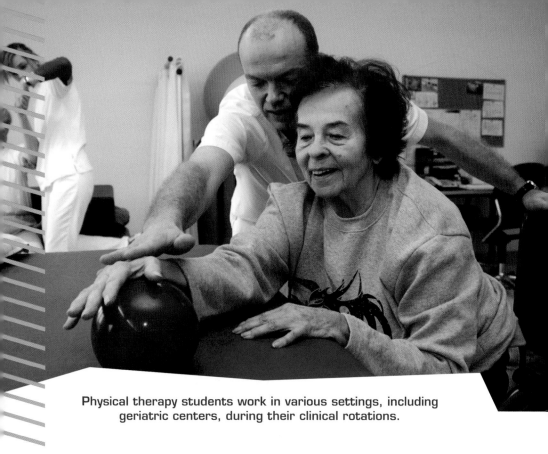

Physical therapy students work in various settings, including geriatric centers, during their clinical rotations.

work under the guidance of a physical therapist in various settings, such as hospitals, rehabilitation centers, pediatric and geriatric centers, private practices, and therapy programs for the homebound.

Professional physical therapist education programs lead to a master's degree (two or more years after a bachelor's degree) or a doctoral degree (three or more years after a bachelor's degree). The reason for this is that the amount of material specific to physical therapy cannot fit comfortably into a bachelor's program. Master's degree programs and doctoral physical therapy programs require students to enter with a bachelor's degree in physical therapy. It takes between six and nine semesters to complete each degree program. More and more physical therapists are entering the field with doctoral degrees.

During your degree work, you'll want to explore as many settings as possible for your future practice. Do you want to work in a private practice or in a large institution? Do you want to work in the city or in the country? Does one specialty attract you?

DOCTOR OF PHYSICAL THERAPY

More physical therapists are graduating with doctoral degrees in physical therapy (DPT). According to the American Physical Therapy Association, in 2008, more than 75 percent of physical therapy students achieved a DPT. And of the 210 accredited physical therapy programs in the United States, 92 percent currently offer a DPT degree.[2]

After you graduate, you must pass a national exam to acquire your license to practice.

Pharmacists work with pharmacist technicians in pharmacies.

WHAT IS A PHARMACIST?

Pharmacy is one of the oldest forms of medical care. Even the most primitive societies knew that various plants, herbs, and minerals had the power to heal or to kill. In those societies, healers often wielded considerable power and influence. A few centuries ago, pharmacists were known as apothecaries. They mixed their own medications from raw ingredients.

Today, pharmacists are still trained to do compounding, which is the mixing of ingredients to create medications, when necessary.

Perhaps your only contact with a pharmacist has been to pick up a prescription at your local drugstore. Besides dispensing prescription drugs, pharmacists also advise patients, physicians, and other health practitioners on the selection, dosages, and side effects of medications. Pharmacists also scrutinize how a patient's various medications will interact with each other, and watch the health and progress of those patients to ensure they are using their medications safely and effectively. Pharmacists must understand the use, effects, and composition of drugs, including their chemical, biological, and physical properties.

One of the most important things pharmacists do is keep good records of their patients' health statuses and the therapies being used to treat them. There are two big

PHARAOH'S PHARMACISTS

Ancient Egyptians used various herbs and other natural ingredients in healing. One cure involved placing an onion in a cut made in the patient's skin. When the sick person could smell the onion, it meant he was improving. A remedy for the common cold was milk taken from a mother who was nursing a son. Other medicines used ingredients such as cumin, caraway, salt, eggs, fat, and honey.

COUNTING THE COSTS

When people don't take their medicine, or when they take the wrong medicine, the economy suffers as well as the patient. The American Pharmacists Association estimates that American businesses lose 20 million workdays per year from mistakes related to medications for heart and circulatory diseases. And many of those mistakes result in hospitalization, costing $8.5 billion.[1]

reasons for this. If the pharmacist knows all the drugs and dosages being used to treat a patient, the pharmacist can spot potentially harmful interactions if new drugs are introduced. Also, misuse of medications is a very common problem, especially with the elderly who might not understand a doctor's instructions. When a pharmacist notices that a medication is repeatedly being refilled sooner than needed, the pharmacist will notify the prescribing doctor and inquire if the prescription has been changed.

Pharmacists are especially vigilant when it comes to narcotic medications. Narcotics are drugs used to relieve severe pain, and many are addictive. Not only do pharmacists notify the prescribing doctor, but they also notify neighboring drugstores. The drugstores will make a record and watch for patients who go to different pharmacies to refill their prescriptions. A pharmacist will also notify the US Drug Enforcement Administration if he or she feels that the ordering doctor has a habit of prescribing a large quantity of narcotic medication.

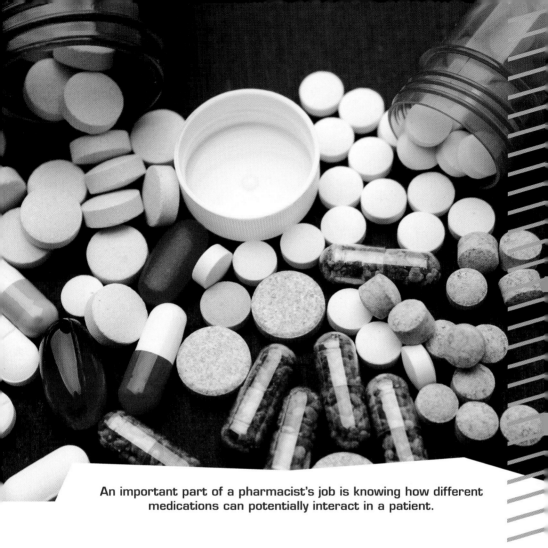

An important part of a pharmacist's job is knowing how different medications can potentially interact in a patient.

WHAT IS A PHARMACIST'S WORK ENVIRONMENT?

Most pharmacists work in retail pharmacies, hospitals, or other medical facilities. The two most important tools of a pharmacist today are the telephone and the computer. Special software not only keeps pharmacists abreast of the latest research and patient information but also provides

WHY IS MEDICINE SO EXPENSIVE?

Pharmaceutical companies are constantly looking for and testing new compounds, but only approximately one in 1,000 finally makes it to the drugstore. First the drug is tested on healthy volunteers to learn about any side effects. Next it is tested on people with the condition for which the drug is targeted to learn about the drug's effectiveness. Finally, before being approved, the medicine is tested on large numbers of patients with and without the condition, to prove that it really works. The whole process takes between 12 and 15 years and costs between $800 million and $1.7 billion.[3]

business tools to help a pharmacy stay efficient and profitable.

Pharmacies are clean, well-lit, and well-ventilated spaces. Pharmacists may need to wear latex gloves, masks, or other protective clothing if working with drugs that need to be kept sterile or are dangerous to touch or inhale. Many pharmacists are on their feet for most of the workday.

Most pharmacists work 40 hours a week, but approximately 19 percent of them work part-time.[2] A benefit of this profession is being able to negotiate one's work schedule. For example, a pharmacist may work ten-hour shifts four days a week. Many community and hospital pharmacies are open for extended hours, so pharmacists may be required to work nights, weekends, and holidays.

Career options for pharmacists have expanded in recent years. While many pharmacists work in retail settings, jobs in pharmacy can be found in a variety of settings. Consultant pharmacists monitor patients' drug therapies at different medical facilities. Some pharmacists specialize in different areas of pharmacy. They may, for example, focus on cancer drugs or on medications used to treat mental disorders. Pharmaceutical companies also employ pharmacists to research, develop, and test new medications. Other settings where pharmacists are needed include health insurance companies, public health care, and educational institutions. Pharmacists work in places you might not expect, as well. You can find pharmacists on cruise ships, at missionary hospitals in Africa, and at Yellowstone National Park.

HOW IS THE JOB MARKET FOR PHARMACISTS?

Pharmacist positions are growing in number. The US Bureau of Labor Statistics predicts they will grow by 17 percent between 2008 and 2018.[4] In 2009, CNN.Money.com rated being a pharmacist the thirteenth best job in the United States.[5] Special expertise and high demand mean that pharmacy is financially rewarding as well. In 2008, there were 269,900 pharmacists employed in the United States, with an average annual wage of $106,410.[6]

According to the American Pharmacists Association, the field of pharmacy is expanding its role within the medical delivery system from just dispensing medication to offering a wide range of services to patients. The association is excited about new ways pharmacists can interact even more helpfully with patients, such as making house calls or devising better ways to keep track of patients' medications.

Pharmacists have a communication advantage over doctors and nurses. Because pharmacists are usually easier and cheaper for patients to contact, they tend to see pharmacists more regularly. The more closely pharmacists work with other medical professionals, the better advice they can give. Pharmacists also administer immunizations, such as the flu vaccine.

A PROFILE OF A PHARMACIST

Eddie Cash is a pharmacist with a Target pharmacy. He was always interested in chemistry and biological sciences in high school. He thought about becoming a doctor, but he did not want to spend the years of schooling needed for that career. Instead, he chose pharmacy.

Cash joined the retail chain right after getting his pharmacy degree and license. He works a 45-hour week, filling prescriptions and counseling customers on their medications. "Something that separates retail pharmacists from other health care resources is that we're free," Cash explained, "so a lot of people come in to ask advice about over-the-counter medicines."[7]

Retail pharmacy work is sometimes stressful, and the hours can seem long, Cash says. It's important to be part of a team that works well together. The human interaction is the part of Cash's job that he likes the best. The part he dislikes is when that interaction doesn't go well. Those situations often involve insurance and billing. He said,

People aren't feeling well, they may not understand their insurance coverage, and the copay is more than they expect. And the pharmacist is the messenger; they can't contact their insurance company. So they may vent at the pharmacist. I try to remind myself that it's not really me they're upset with, but I'm the only person they can talk to.[8]

Cash confirms that every pharmacist encounters forged prescriptions and "doctor-shopping." This is when a prescription may be legal, but the customer has obtained simultaneous prescriptions for the same medication from numerous doctors. Pharmacists quickly learn to spot these maneuvers.

Cash believes the most important qualities in a successful pharmacist are an interest in

MOST PRESCRIBED DRUGS IN 2008 IN THE UNITED STATES

1. Hydrocodone (with acetaminophen): Used to treat pain.

2. Lisinopril: For hypertension (high blood pressure).

3. Simvastatin: For high cholesterol.

4. Levothyroxine: For hypothyroidism (a condition where the thyroid under-produces growth hormones).

5. Amoxicillin: For bacterial infection.

6. Azithromycin: For bacterial infection.

7. Lipitor: For high cholesterol.

8. Hydrochlorothiazide: For edema/hypertension (high blood pressure).

9. Alprazolam: For anxiety and depression.

10. Atenolol: For hypertension (high blood pressure).[9]

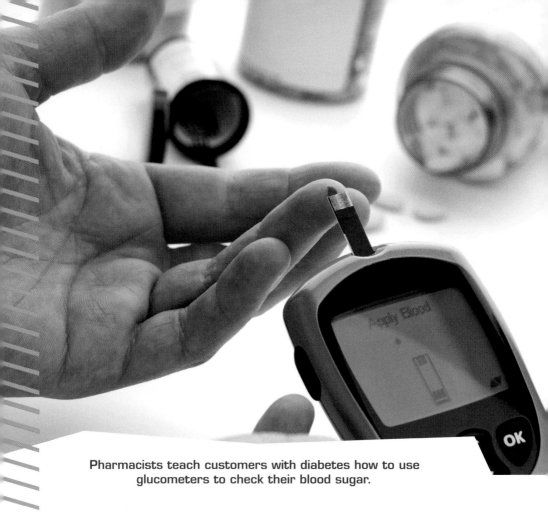

Pharmacists teach customers with diabetes how to use glucometers to check their blood sugar.

science and being detail-orientated. "Most of us are a little obsessive-compulsive in different areas of the job," he said with a smile. "But that's a good thing. It means we'll serve the customer better."[10]

A DAY IN THE LIFE OF A PHARMACIST

A typical day for a pharmacist varies depending on where the pharmacist works. In a retail pharmacy, a day will involve one-on-one communication with customers. Many customers are elderly people taking several medicines. Every new prescription needs to be checked for accuracy, appropriateness, and interactions with other medications.

The pharmacy also carries equipment that pharmacists may have to teach patients how to use—everything from crutches to nebulizers (a device that sprays liquid into a fine mist so it can be inhaled) to blood sugar testing kits, or glucometers. A retail pharmacist also spends a good amount of time on the phone with doctors' offices verifying prescriptions and with insurance companies trying to understand patients' coverage.

A retail pharmacist usually depends on one or more pharmacy technicians. The technicians prepare prescriptions with the aid of computer programs. The pharmacist then rechecks each order before it is rung up for the patient by the clerk.

A research pharmacist has a very different typical day from a retail pharmacist. Most likely, a research pharmacist works alone or with a team of researchers that could include doctors, nurses, statisticians, and other professionals interested in the research being conducted. While most of the day is spent working independently, some time is spent in meetings or brainstorming sessions with other researchers. Depending on the research, pharmacists may be working on new and exciting medical solutions to cancer, depression, or other diseases. While research pharmacists have little, if any, direct contact with patients, they know that the medication they research could possibly affect the lives of many patients.

TOP FIVE QUESTIONS ABOUT BECOMING A PHARMACIST

1. *How long do I have to go to school?*

   Being a pharmacist requires a doctoral degree from an accredited pharmacy school. To be admitted to a pharmacy school, you must have completed two to four years of college, studying science and math, in particular. After that, it will take you four years to earn a doctoral degree.

2. *What are the benefits of being a pharmacist?*

   Pharmacists have contact with more people than most other medical professionals. They know that their work benefits the health of many patients. This is probably one of the best parts of the job! Pharmacists are needed almost everywhere, and they can usually arrange a schedule that suits them. Salaries are also high for pharmacists.

3. *What are some negative aspects of being a pharmacist?*

   Very few pharmacists enjoy the paperwork required in dealing with insurance companies. And while most pharmacists say customer contact is the thing they love the best about their jobs, not every customer reinforces that feeling. Customers who are rude and unreasonable also come with the territory.

4. *Are pharmacists satisfied with their jobs?*
   Pharmacists mostly love their work. They get
   frustrated at things that keep them from doing the
   work they enjoy as well as possible. According to
   CNN.Money.com, being a pharmacist ranked ninth
   out of the 50 best jobs in the United States.[11]

5. *What qualities does a pharmacist absolutely require?*
   They must be prepared and have the desire to attend
   school for many years to achieve the degrees needed
   to be a pharmacist. Pharmacists need to pay constant
   attention to detail. Communication skills are also
   important, as pharmacists must be able to translate
   complicated medical terminology and instructions
   into language that patients can easily understand and
   follow. To be a good research pharmacist, you must
   be able to work well independently and have strong
   commitment to your research specialty.

Good communication skills are needed for pharmacists to relay instructions to patients.

WOULD YOU MAKE A GOOD PHARMACIST?

Pharmacists almost always say that the most important skill their profession requires is the ability to deal with people. A pharmacist needs great communication skills, including the ability to listen.

HAVING EMPATHY

Just about any list of qualities necessary in medical professions will include empathy. Empathy isn't the same as sympathy. You can feel sorry for someone without having any understanding of that person's particular situation. Empathetic people will try to put themselves in their patients' shoes to remember from their own experiences how it feels to be confused, in pain, or worried.

ISAAC NEWTON, APPRENTICE PHARMACIST

Sir Isaac Newton (1643–1727) changed the world with his theory of gravity. He served as an apprentice apothecary, or pharmacist's aide, in Grantham, England, living with the town's apothecary. He left to study at Cambridge, where he began his illustrious career in physics and mathematics.

DETAILS AND ORGANIZATION

Pharmacists need to be detail-oriented people. One pharmacist described the daily work of a pharmacist:

> You're going to be checking hundreds of prescriptions a day. Each prescription needs to be checked in detail.

> Do you have the right patient, the right drug, dosage form, directions, and strength?

> You have five patients in line. Are all the prescriptions separated so as to not get mixed up?

In short, it's a complicated environment and it helps if you are a detail-oriented person.[1]

If you aren't naturally tidy, orderly, or organized—basically a neat freak—you'll need to develop those qualities to be a pharmacist. You may think pharmacy isn't brain surgery, but in both professions, mistakes can be fatal.

CHECKLIST

Is pharmacy right for you? Take a look at this checklist to see if this career is a good fit.

- *Are you usually neat and well organized?*

- *Do you have a good memory?*

- *Do you enjoy chemistry and biology?*

- *Are you patient when people are difficult?*

- *Do you like helping others?*

- *Are you skilled at verbally communicating instructions?*

If you answered yes to most of these questions, you already have some of the qualities that make a good pharmacist. If you answered no to some, don't worry. If you still want to be a pharmacist, hard work and determination will go a long way.

HOW TO GET THERE

HIGH SCHOOL

Take Advanced Placement science classes if they are available and graduate with your best possible grades. You can also work as a pharmacy aide. Pharmacy aides do administrative work in pharmacies. They may answer phones, stock shelves, and operate cash registers. It is great experience in a pharmacy setting, which will help you prepare to be a pharmacist.

COLLEGE AND BEYOND

Being a pharmacist requires a doctoral degree from a pharmacy school that has been approved by the Accreditation Council for Pharmacy Education. Some students enter a four-year college with a pharmacy school directly from high school and are able to complete their doctoral degree in six years. Some students enter pharmacy school with a two-year associate's degree from a community college. Still other students get a four-year degree or more

HARMFUL RESULTS WITH COMMON DRUGS

Incorrectly combining drugs can cause dangerous reactions. Approximately 2.2 million older adults in the United States take their medicine incorrectly. According to a study by researchers at the University of Chicago Medical Center, these interactions can cause gastrointestinal bleeding, muscle breakdown, disruption in heart rhythm, and other serious problems. Half of the interactions involve over-the-counter medications, such as aspirin or dietary supplements. Knowing how drugs interact is a vital part of a pharmacist's job.[2]

Working as a clerk in a pharmacy provides valuable experience.

and then go into a pharmacy program at another school for another four years. Pharmacy programs will require you to have taken courses in mathematics, chemistry, biology, physics, humanities, and social sciences.

By the time you have your degree, hopefully, you'll have explored the huge variety of pharmacy job settings. Once licensed, you could go right to work in a retail pharmacy or hospital pharmacy. There are one- or two-year residency programs where pharmacists can receive specialized training. Some pharmacy graduates decide to combine their training with a law degree. Having a law degree may be good for a pharmacist who wants to work on pharmaceutical patents in a law firm.

HERBAL MEDICINE

As you can tell by looking in any health food store, people still treat medical conditions with plants, seeds, roots, leaves, and flowers. While most people view herbal medicine to be outside the realm of conventional medicine, many prescription and over-the-counter drugs originated with plants and herbs. An obvious example is aspirin, which originally came from willow bark. Its active ingredient, acetylsalicylic acid, has now been purified and concentrated by aspirin manufacturers.

Neonatal nurses work in a hospital's neonatal intensive care unit.

WHAT IS A NEONATAL NURSE?

What is the most dramatic department in the hospital? You might guess it's the emergency room. But for emotional ups and downs, life-or-death crises, what television might call raw human drama, it's tough to beat the maternity ward.

The birth of a baby is usually a happy, long-awaited event. It also comes with pain and an array of dangers and surprises that can turn celebration into tragedy. Every birth is unique, but the constant in the maternity ward is the care and skill of the neonatal nurse.

FLORENCE NIGHTINGALE

Florence Nightingale (1820–1910), an English woman, laid the foundations of professional nursing. International Nurses Day is celebrated around the world on her birthday, May 12.

She came to prominence for her pioneering work in nursing during the Crimean War (1853–1856), where she tended to wounded soldiers. She once said, "For it may safely be said, not that the habit of ready and correct observation will by itself make us useful nurses, but that without it we shall be useless with all our devotion."[1]

Neonatal nurses care for mothers giving birth and for newborn babies in hospitals during the first 28 days of life. Some neonatal nurses may be in the delivery room. During labor, they monitor the vital signs of the mother and the baby and watch for any signs of difficulty. They may coach mothers during labor. They may assist during surgeries involved in labor, such as caesarean sections or episiotomies. When the baby is born, they wash the baby and take a blood sample. The sample and the nurse's observations help doctors and staff determine if the baby needs special care or further testing.

Hospitals usually identify three levels of newborn care. Level I neonatal nurses care for healthy, full-term or near-

HOSPITAL-BASED NURSING PROGRAMS

While most registered nurses (RNs) earn their degrees at college or university nursing schools, a few hospitals offer their own nurse training programs. Students in programs such as these train for two or three years to receive their RN certificate. Some programs accept high school graduates with no nursing experience. Others train RNs in specialties. One advantage to a hospital nursing school is the clinical setting and the opportunity to view a variety of specialties up close. Students who do well in these programs may also be at an advantage for job opportunities in the hospital where they've studied.

term babies. Level II neonatal nurses care for premature and seriously ill babies who need constant supervision. Level III neonatal intensive care unit (NICU) nurses care for very sick and very premature infants. Nurses in levels II and III provide more in-depth care for newborns. This includes tube or bottle feeding the babies; using high-tech equipment, such as ventilators or incubators; and providing education to parents about caring for their premature or ill child.

WHAT IS A NEONATAL NURSE'S WORK ENVIRONMENT?

Neonatal nurses work in well-lit and busy hospital environments. The maternity ward includes a central desk (where nurses can do paperwork), birthing rooms, and rooms for mothers recovering from childbirth. When not with their mothers, healthy newborn infants are cared for in a nursery.

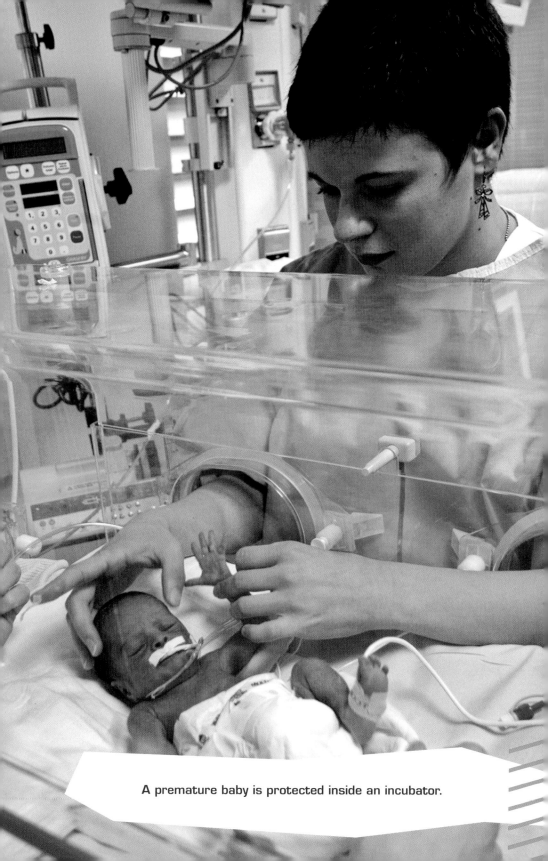

A premature baby is protected inside an incubator.

The sounds a nurse hears include mothers in childbirth, the bustle of medical personnel, and the cries of healthy newborns. You probably won't hear crying in the NICU, though—many of the babies aren't yet healthy enough to make a lot of noise.

The NICU is also filled with the beeping and sighing of high-tech machines, automatic alarms going off, and the bustle of doctors and nurses discussing or attending to their fragile patients. The babies, many weighing less than two pounds (0.9 kg), lie in incubators. Many are attached to breathing or intravenous tubes.

Many NICU nurses work eight- or 12-hour shifts, but the babies don't follow a schedule. Many neonatal nurses have found themselves staying well beyond their shifts because of crises with their patients.

NEONATAL INCUBATORS

Inside the NICU, incubators are one of the essential tools used to keep premature babies alive. Premature infants do not have enough body fat to keep warm, may have undeveloped lungs or organs, and are susceptible to catching viruses and germs. Incubators are enclosed environments for babies, keeping them warm, oxygenated, hydrated, and safe. Neonatal nurses constantly monitor their tiny patients' health using incubators, ventilators, and other devices.

HOW IS THE JOB MARKET FOR NEONATAL NURSES?

According to the US Bureau of Labor Statistics, registered nurses made up the largest medical occupation in

2008, with 2.6 million jobs. Hospitals employed 60 percent of registered nurses (RNs). The remaining 40 percent are employed in physician's offices, home health care services, nursing care facilities, employment services, social services, government agencies, and educational institutions.

Although salaries for RNs vary depending on specialties, experience, and the community, the yearly salary for RNs ranges from $51,640 to $76,570.[2] Salaries of neonatal nurses range between $50,421 and $82,975 per year.[3]

The career outlook for neonatal nurses is good. The US Bureau of Labor Statistics estimates that the need for registered nurses will continue to rise faster than average through 2018. Continuing advances in fertility treatments are allowing more women to become

CLARA BARTON, RED CROSS FOUNDER

Perhaps the most famous nurse in US history is Clara Barton (1821–1912), who was known by soldiers in the American Civil War (1861–1865) as the "Angel of the Battlefield." Born in Massachusetts, she quit her job in the US Patent Office in Washington DC because the administration favored slavery. When Abraham Lincoln was elected president, she returned to Washington. When the Civil War started, Clara began nursing the wounded Union soldiers and bringing supplies to battle sites.

After the war, Barton went around the country lecturing about her experiences. In 1869, her health began to fail and she took a vacation in Europe. There, she became involved with the International Red Cross, and when she returned to the United States, she set about convincing the federal government to establish a Red Cross. She succeeded in 1882 and was head of the US Red Cross for 23 years.

mothers, including older women, who may require more nursing care in the maternity ward. NICU nurses will also be in high demand. According to the March of Dimes, there are approximately 530,000 babies born prematurely each year in the United States.[4]

A PROFILE OF A NEONATAL NURSE

Elizabeth Lopez is a NICU nurse at Duke University Hospital in Durham, North Carolina. A typical 12-hour shift for her begins with a briefing from nurses on the previous shift. The briefing covers the babies' conditions and current medications and highlights any changes or special instructions. She assesses the babies under her care two or three times in the course of her shift. She said,

> One of the things I appreciate about my job is being an integral part of a health care team that includes doctors and nurse practitioners (NPs). The doctors rely on the nurses' observations; if we notice something, they pay attention.[5]

The NICU where Lopez works is extremely high-tech. Lopez doesn't find that intimidating, though. "I worked in an adult ICU before this, so some of the monitoring equipment is the same," she said. "The new stuff—and some of it is really advanced— you learn by doing."[6] Lopez's hospital offers a 26-week internship for nurses hoping to specialize in level III care of infants.

Lopez said that the best part of her job is being there for people, the families as well as the babies. "Sometimes we can

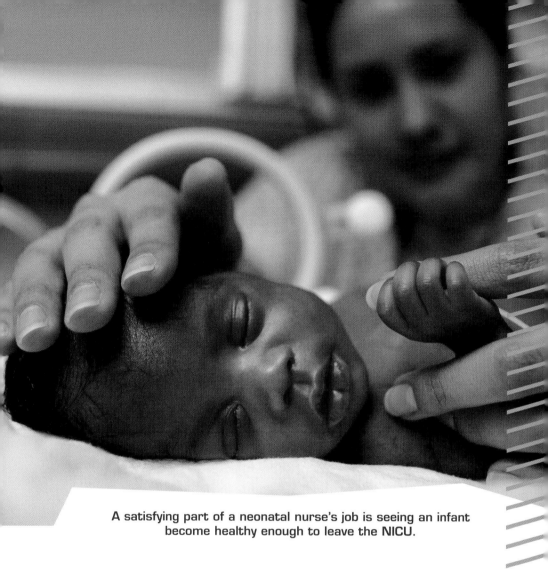

A satisfying part of a neonatal nurse's job is seeing an infant become healthy enough to leave the **NICU**.

make the babies better, sometimes we can't," she said. "But we're with families at the best and worst times in their lives, and at those times a nurse can make such a difference!"[7] The worst part of the job for Lopez, predictably, is when a baby dies. "But we save a lot of them," she explained, "so I try to remember that, and also to remember that the babies in the NICU are a small number, less than 10 percent, of all the babies the hospital treats."[8] She finds it sad that many of the babies on level III are there because of their parents' addictions; the infants may have fetal alcohol syndrome, AIDS, or are addicted to drugs.

Lopez believes certain qualities are necessary in neonatal nursing. "You need compassion and empathy," she said, "but you also need the skills. You can be incredibly busy, but you can't take shortcuts that will make a difference in care."[9]

Brigit Carter is a colleague of Lopez's at Duke. She has been a NICU nurse for 12 years. She recently completed her doctorate. "I'm teaching now," she says, "but I love working with the babies and their families too much to let it go completely, so I still work part-time in the NICU."[10]

When asked about the best and worst parts of her job, Carter says the two are intertwined. "The work is intense and stressful," she says. "And it's wonderful to see a child who comes to us so incredibly fragile go home to live a normal life. But when that doesn't happen, and a family needs to say goodbye, you can give them all they need to make that transition."[11] Carter remembers losing a baby she treated for nine months. "It's sad, really hard," she says.[12] But she stays in touch with the families whatever the outcome. At the holidays, she gets cards of thanks and photos of some of the children she's cared for.

She believes the most important qualities in a level III neonatal nurse are focus, attention to detail, compassion, and "a sincere desire to be there. You have to love what you're doing."[13]

A DAY IN THE LIFE OF A NEONATAL NURSE

On a typical day, a neonatal nurse may care for three to four babies. At the start of each shift, the neonatal nurse receives the patients' status reports. The nurse then checks orders and sends out formulas for the babies' first feeds. The nurse may give baths to the patients as well. Newborn babies eat frequently—every two to three hours—so soon it is time for another feeding for the babies. Changing diapers and soothing distressed babies is also a big part of the job. In between feedings, changings, and baths, neonatal nurses teach parents how to feed and care for their babies. There are also visitors who come in to visit each baby, so a neonatal nurse's duties must be scheduled around these visits.

Depending on the baby's illness or issue, the neonatal nurse monitors various machines or equipment attached to the baby. These can include an IV or feeding tube, a ventilator, or an incubator. The babies may be recovering from surgery and a nurse will have to care for their surgical incisions. Nurses constantly check the vital statistics of their patients. Critically ill patients may need to be checked every 15 minutes, while more stable patients are checked every hour.

Toward the end of a shift, a neonatal nurse will record the patients' statuses in their medical charts. The nurse may change each baby's bed and then restock the stations by each baby. Before the end of the shift, the leaving nurse must update incoming nurses on each patient.

TOP FIVE QUESTIONS ABOUT BECOMING A NEONATAL NURSE

1. *How long do I have to go to school?*

   To become a neonatal nurse, you must have both an undergraduate and master's degree. Between degrees, a neonatal nurse usually completes two years of clinical work. After achieving a master's degree, a neonatal nurse needs to pass a certification exam. Then throughout a neonatal nurse's career, continuing education is usually required.

2. *What are the benefits of being a neonatal nurse?*

   You have a chance to help babies and their families in a very personal way. You are there during some of the happiest moments in people's lives and some of the saddest. You can live just about anywhere. The need for nurses, including neonatal nurses, is everywhere.

3. *What are some negative aspects of being a neonatal nurse?*

   The job can be stressful, especially when you're just starting out. Nursing is physically demanding. You are on your feet for long hours. Birth is risky and things can go wrong. You have to deal with your own grief when patients (babies or mothers) die.

4. *Are neonatal nurses satisfied with their jobs?*
    One of the most satisfying parts of being a neonatal
    nurse is seeing positive outcomes from their patients.
    When a struggling premature infant is finally healthy
    enough to go home with happy parents, it makes a
    neonatal nurse feel great. According to a study in
    Pediatric Nursing, neonatal nurses also enjoy the level
    of income they receive, the team spirit among the
    other nurses, the respect they receive, and the support
    they receive from physicians.[14]

5. *What qualities does a neonatal nurse absolutely require?*
    A neonatal nurse needs to have a desire to help
    others and have a love for babies. Good observational
    skills are also necessary. Emergency situations often
    occur in the NICU, so having the ability to stay calm
    under stressful situations is valuable. Being able
    to communicate well with frightened and stressed
    parents helps ease their concerns. Patience and
    having a supportive nature are also good qualities to
    have as a neonatal nurse.

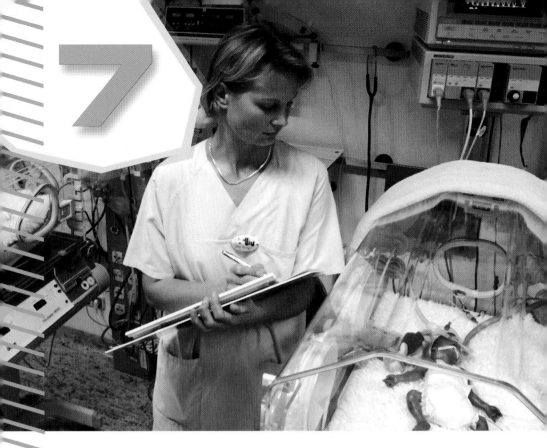

Neonatal nurses must keep track of every detail related to their patients' health.

WOULD YOU MAKE A GOOD NEONATAL NURSE?

A neonatal nurse probably has a soft spot for babies. Maybe you're lucky enough to have a baby in your family. If so, do you like taking care of the baby? Have you earned extra money babysitting for families with babies?

Does your high school have a child development class, the kind where they send you home with an electronic baby to care for? If you haven't taken it, give it a try. Babies are cute, but they are also demanding, even—or maybe especially—when they are healthy.

ATTENTION TO THE DETAILS

How observant are you? Nurses are trained to recognize and respond to the signs they see in their patients. Observation is especially important as a neonatal nurse, since babies cannot explain to you how they feel.

Much of a neonatal nurse's work involves attention to routine and detail. A nurse collects and analyzes data about his or her patients in a systematic way. Neonatal nurses need to be organized. You will have several patients at once and several treatment plans to implement. The plans have specific schedules that need to be followed. At the same time, you may need to respond to unexpected crises. If you are good at managing your schoolwork, extra-curricular activities, and chores at home,

MIRACLE BABY

The world's smallest baby boy was born in Göttingen hospital in Germany in June 2009. He weighed 9.7 ounces (275 g) and was delivered by caesarean section at 25 weeks old.[1] The baby was kept in intensive care and was allowed to go home with his parents in March 2010.[2]

COUNSELING NEW MOTHERS

Neonatal nurses work with new mothers to facilitate breastfeeding. The advantages of breastfeeding over bottle-feeding are significant. Breastfeeding builds immunity and resistance to infection and has superior nutritional benefits. The act of breastfeeding also includes skin-to-skin contact between mother and child. This creates an important bond that is delayed due to the infant being separated from the mother in the NICU. According to the National Association of Neonatal Nurses, breastfeeding should start within the first 24 hours after an infant is born.

that ability will help you as a nurse.

LEARNING FOR LIFE

For as long as you practice nursing, you will need to continue educating yourself about new technologies and procedures. As with most professions in medicine, an interest and aptitude in science are important. One neonatal nurse described her work:

The role encompasses everything I loved learning in nursing school: high-tech [equipment], being involved in and utilizing research, providing critical care, creative problem-solving, increased autonomy, working with many disciplines, and most of all, working with parents and their new babies.[3]

HANDLING EMOTIONS

How do you handle emotion? Can you remain calm when people around you are in pain, dealing with a crisis, or are grieving? It's not a good idea to hold everything inside.

But there are times when a nurse needs to be a rock for patients—empathetic and caring, but strong.

CHECKLIST

Is neonatal nursing right for you? Take a look at this checklist to see if this career is a good fit.

- *Do you like to be neat and well organized?*

- *Do people tell you that you're a good listener?*

- *Do you notice changes in people's appearance or mood?*

- *Do you enjoy science and math?*

- *Does helping others make you feel good?*

- *Do you remain calm when people around you are going crazy?*

If you answered yes to all of the above, you have qualities that will truly help you in neonatal nursing. If you answered no to one or more, don't worry. These are all qualities you can develop if you work on them.

HOW TO GET THERE

HIGH SCHOOL

In school, you will want to maintain a high grade point average, especially in chemistry, biology, math, and health courses. Many high schools now offer child development

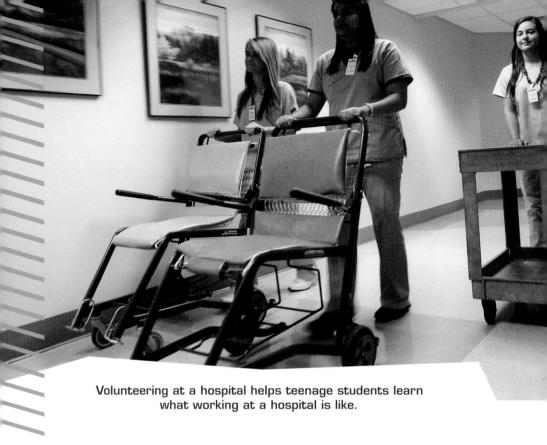
Volunteering at a hospital helps teenage students learn what working at a hospital is like.

courses that include caring for a computerized "baby" at home. You also might ask your school counselor if your school is affiliated with Health Occupations Students of America (HOSA). The mission of HOSA is to provide opportunities for knowledge, skill, and leadership development for all health science technology education students.

VOLUNTEER EXPERIENCE

Students who are interested in the medical field often find volunteering or job shadowing at a hospital beneficial. Hospitals accept volunteers of different ages, so check with the hospitals in your area to see if they accept volunteers your age. Volunteers may assist staff in patient care and provide information and service to families or to patients. Volunteers may work in hospital offices. Most hospitals require a time commitment of a few hours a week over a period of several months. Some programs may tailor a volunteer's work to his or her special interests or skills.

You'll need to complete an application, interview for the position, probably produce a teacher reference, and pass a criminal background check. Every program is different, but you can go to the Web site of a hospital near you for more specific information.

COLLEGE AND BEYOND

Neonatal nurses start as registered nurses. A nursing student must complete a bachelor's degree program in nursing at a college or university or a nursing program at a hospital. During college, many nursing students volunteer at local hospitals or with medical providers as nurse's assistants. To become a neonatal nurse,

"What the neonatologist knows is that even the best engineering sometimes fails. The slightest misstep along the way, in the formation of the heart or the plates of the skull or the closure of the palate or the structure of the abdominal wall, and the baby becomes a NICU patient. . . . In the NICU, the vexing question of when life begins, which has sparked so much anger and debate, pales next to the far more practical question of when survival can be imagined. Or should be."[4]

—*Edward Humes*, Baby ER

it is important to take elective courses or specialize in labor and delivery during your nursing education.

SHORTAGES EASING

According to a report released in July 2010 by the Tri-Council for Nursing, the economic recession has led to nursing shortages easing in parts of the country. But they believe this is only temporary. The council believes that the demand for nursing services will increase in the coming years.

It is also possible to become an RN by getting an associate's degree at a community college. For positions of increased responsibility, a bachelor's degree is often required. Many colleges and universities around the country offer registered nurse degrees. Students must then pass a national licensing examination called the NCLEX-RN. Once they pass, they become registered nurses who are allowed to practice.

After college, most nurses do two years of clinical work in a NICU. They then enter a graduate degree program in neonatal nursing, which will include more course work and clinical work. When you have your master's degree, you'll need to pass a certification exam to be certified as a neonatal nurse practitioner.

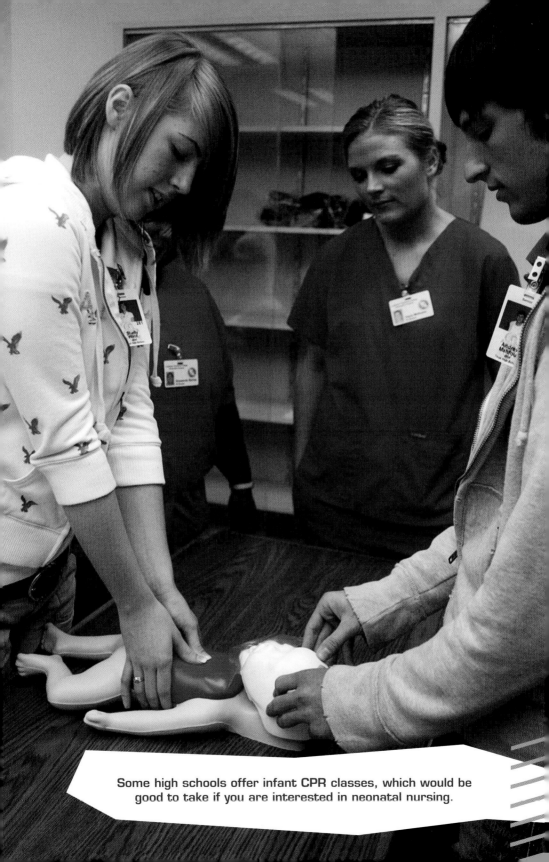

Some high schools offer infant CPR classes, which would be good to take if you are interested in neonatal nursing.

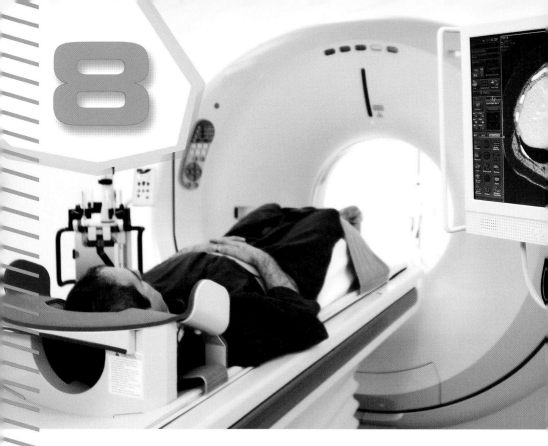

An MRI scan allows a neurosurgeon to see inside a person's skull
without performing an invasive surgical procedure.

WHAT IS A
NEUROSURGEON?

What's in your brain? It can be a little
uncomfortable to think about. Everything
you know, everything you experience, your memories, your
wishes, and your identity—you—all depend on a roughly

three-pound (1.4-kg) organ between your ears. Your brain is a marvel, and in many ways, it is a mystery.

Imagine opening up a person's skull and cutting into that mystery in order to save or improve a life. This is called neurosurgery. Neurosurgeons operate on the brain, the spine, and the nerves. A tiny sampling of health issues they treat include trauma, tumors and cysts, epilepsy, birth defects, bleeding or infections in the brain, and damaged discs in the spine.

Often, even with the best surgical treatments, patients suffering from brain injuries fail to recover 100 percent of their function. Other times, neurosurgeons will discover that a cancerous tumor can't be completely removed, and they will have to explain to a patient that his or her condition is terminal.

MALPRACTICE

If you become a neurosurgeon, the odds are good that you may be sued for malpractice. Malpractice is the improper or negligent treatment of a patient. For example, if a doctor incorrectly operates on a patient and that patient is permanently disabled because of the surgery, the patient may sue the doctor for malpractice.

Spinal operations account for almost two-thirds of all neurosurgical operations in the United States. These operations cover a wide range as well, from repairing a ruptured disc or fusing vertebrae, to attempting to repair or limit an injury that could cause death or paralysis.

A neurosurgeon can take one of several career paths. Some go into private practice, on their own or as part of

SPINAL SURGERY

A 2006 survey by the American Association of Neurological Surgeons found that spine-related surgery made up nearly 62 percent of the total number of operations performed by neurosurgeons. The most common surgery was lumbar disc laminectomy, a procedure that treats spinal stenosis. Spinal stenosis is a narrowing of the lower spinal canal that can occur with aging, and may cause pain or numbness by pressing on the spinal nerve.[1]

a group. Other neurosurgeons continue their education, becoming experts in even more specialized fields such as cerebrovascular and skull base surgery (which treats blood vessels in the brain and medical problems at the base of the skull), endovascular neurosurgery (the treatment of complex neurovascular diseases, such as aneurysms and arteriovenous malformations), the surgical treatment of Parkinson's disease, neuro-oncology (the treatment of cancer and tumors of the brain and nervous system), neurotrauma, and pediatric neurosurgery. Some neurosurgeons go on to teach in medical school or do laboratory research.

WHAT IS A NEUROSURGEON'S WORK ENVIRONMENT?

In a bright and sterile operating room, a neurosurgeon depends on a team of medical professionals. An anesthesiologist monitors a patient's consciousness, breathing, and heart rate. A surgical technician supplies the

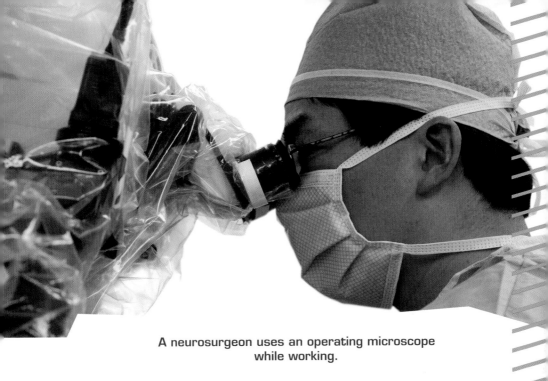

A neurosurgeon uses an operating microscope
while working.

tools needed for the operation. Assisting surgeons may open the patient for the procedure and close the patient after the operation or procedure.

Neurosurgeons work with some amazing high-tech equipment. Take, for example, the gamma knife. It is a machine that can destroy some brain tumors with radiation from outside the skull. Imaging techniques such as magnetic resonance imaging (MRI), which can show detailed pictures of internal organs, also continue to advance. Neurosurgeons need to be able to read MRI scans to see how, where, and whether to operate on a patient. Modern imaging techniques have been a wonderful gift to neurosurgeons, allowing them to map out operations before surgery.

Neurosurgeons learn and practice their specialty during their hospital residency, which lasts approximately six years.

Resident neurosurgeons treat patients only when they are in the hospital. They may operate on a patient under the supervision of an attending, the patient's actual physician, or be called to treat emergency cases. Either way, the patient is often severely impaired or unconscious when the resident sees him or her. After the surgery, the patient may leave the hospital for home, rehabilitation, or nursing care, and the surgeon never really learns the long-term outcome.

Neurosurgeons in private practices treat emergencies but also have the opportunity to work cases from the beginning. They learn their patients' histories and will follow their patients' progress after the operation or operations. It's not unusual for a patient to require multiple surgeries before a full recovery.

Some neurosurgeons teach in university hospitals. They make rounds with residents, quizzing them about patients' cases, and they supervise surgical procedures

TRENDS IN NEUROSURGERY

According to the American Association of Neurological Surgeons, the changes in neurosurgery between 1999 and 2006 were:

- "A decrease of 14 percent in the number of neurosurgeons in private practice
- A decrease of 13 percent in the number of neurosurgeons in solo practice
- An 11 percent increase in the number of neurosurgeons with full-time academic appointments
- A 6 percent increase in the number of female neurosurgeons"[2]

the residents perform. They may hold this position as an adjunct, meaning they have their own practices in addition to their teaching duties.

HOW IS THE JOB MARKET FOR NEUROSURGEONS?

According to the US Bureau of Labor Statistics, physicians and surgeons in general will see a 22 percent increase in employment from 2008 to 2018.[3] And it's likely, given the continued expansion of health care–related industries and the aging population, that growth will continue beyond that point.

As you might suspect, neurosurgeons are some of the best paid specialists in medicine. In one survey, they reported incomes from $354,000 to $936,000, with an average of $541,000.[4] To put that in perspective, think about the student loans that may need to be paid off after a neurosurgeon's education. The average medical school graduate, before internship or residency, owes more than $150,000 in loans.[5] Neurosurgeons in private practice also pay for their own health insurance, retirement, office rent, and staff. They also have to pay for malpractice insurance. And that insurance is expensive, because neurosurgeons who are sued are frequently sued for large amounts. The reason for this is that a mistake in brain surgery can have such serious consequences for a patient. One well-known neurosurgeon reported in 2006 that, although she had never been sued, her malpractice insurance premium was $106,000 a year.[6]

A PROFILE OF A NEUROSURGEON

Dr. Stephen Boone was a high school student in Texas when a science teacher suggested he consider becoming a doctor. He loved science and was especially fascinated by anatomy. So he enrolled in pre-med at Duke University in North Carolina. At Duke he was elected president of the Pre-Med Society.

"I had thought about going into heart surgery," he recalls, "but one of the speakers I got for our Society meetings was a neurosurgeon, and he really got me interested in that specialty."[7] Boone went on to Duke Medical School and discovered that neuroanatomy was his favorite course. So he went to a professor of neurosurgery and asked if he could work in his lab. When the doctor asked him what kind of work he was interested in, Boone said, "Well sir, I'd like to study transplanting brains."[8]

Boone laughs about that today. He did, however, go to work for the neurosurgeon, studying the peripheral nervous system thoroughly for the rest of his medical school career. At Duke he had also joined the US Army Reserve, and after medical school he was drafted to serve in Vietnam. During the war he was a member of special forces, called the Green Berets.

After the war, Boone did his residency in neurosurgery, then taught at the University of North Carolina in Chapel Hill before going into private practice. Today, he is semiretired and living in Raleigh, North Carolina. During his career, Boone has seen incredible advances in technology, especially in imaging. "That's been wonderful," he says, remembering when neurosurgeons had to depend more or less on skull X-rays and their knowledge of brain anatomy.[9] He remembers occasionally sedating a patient in the X-ray room, then injecting dye into their carotid (neck) arteries to try to get a better presurgical picture of a tumor.

In his practice, Boone has specialized in repairing aneurysms and removing brain tumors, and he is still fascinated by the anatomy of the nervous system. But by far, the best part of his career in neurosurgery, Boone says, has been being able to help people. "When you clip an aneurysm or remove a benign tumor, you really change a person's life for the better," he says, "and that's very gratifying."[10] His least favorite part is the paperwork, which has increased during the course of his career.

OUTWARD IMPRESSION

Neurosurgeon and author Sherwin B. Nuland became acquainted with pediatric neurosurgeon Forrest Harrison when he treated Nuland's daughter. In his book *The Soul of Medicine*, Nuland wrote of his first impression of the doctor, "Like many neurosurgeons, Forrest Harrison cultivates an air—no, call it an aura—of remote superiority. Depending on how well one knows the men, and more recently the women, who have populated this demanding specialty, the aura may be seen as either a genuine cloak of aloofness intended to intimidate colleagues in other fields of medicine or a [shell] of well-disguised protection against the hurts they encounter in their everyday activities. The contents of the skull and spinal column permit few errors, and the smallest hint of fallibility tempts frail tissue toward revenge."[11]

What are the most important qualities for young people considering neurosurgery as a career? "You should want to help people," he says. "It helps to have reasonably good hand coordination and you need average intelligence. You also need stamina," Boone says with a smile. "Operating all night and then having a difficult, delicate case the next day—it helps to be young."[12]

A DAY IN THE LIFE OF A NEUROSURGEON

When a neurosurgeon awakes, often at 5:00 or 6:00 a.m., it might be an office day or a hospital day. In either case, the neurosurgeon is probably facing a ten– to 14-hour day. Neurosurgeons in private practice typically try to see patients in the office some days and schedule surgery at the hospital on others. But if one of their hospital patients suddenly develops complications, their schedule can rapidly change.

Neurosurgeons in private practice often work with a neurosurgery group, sometimes filling in for each other and sharing "on call" time, when they are available for emergencies. A typical schedule may involve two or three days per week in the office, seeing patients and attending to paperwork, with two days for surgery at a hospital with which they are affiliated.

Their office time is split between evaluating new patients and monitoring the postsurgical recovery of patients on whom they've operated. Neurosurgeons are also expected to continue their education by attending scientific meetings and keeping up with professional journals.

Neurosurgeons examine brain scans to learn about their patients' illnesses.

TOP FIVE QUESTIONS ABOUT BECOMING A NEUROSURGEON

1. *How long do I need to go to school?*

   A neurosurgeon goes to college for four years to earn a bachelor's degree and to medical school for another four years to earn an MD. Then, he or she spends six years in residency at a hospital. Formal education continues throughout the career.

2. *What are the benefits of being a neurosurgeon?*

   You can help people in a way very few others can. You are also an explorer; much of the brain is unknown territory. You will be on the cutting edge of scientific discovery of the brain.

3. *What are some negative aspects of being a neurosurgeon?*

   The educational journey is long, demanding, and expensive. You may also have to pay back large amounts of student loans, purchase malpractice insurance, and deal with insurance paperwork. In your practice, you will also encounter health tragedies you are powerless to prevent or cure.

4. *How satisfied are neurosurgeons with their work?*
   Neurosurgeons are at a high risk for burnout. In a
   2009 study on physician job satisfaction, a career as
   a neurological surgeon ranked among the lowest in
   job satisfaction.[13] Some of the reasons cited were the
   irregular hours, malpractice suits, lost autonomy, and
   relative decrease in pay compared to other medical
   specialties. Neurosurgeons also reported that their
   jobs didn't meet the very high career expectations
   they had before entering the field.

5. *What qualities does a neurosurgeon absolutely require?*
   A neurosurgeon possesses curiosity, perseverance, and
   great problem-solving skills. Having the curiosity and
   desire to learn of new developments in neurosurgery
   is also necessary. Brain surgery can be complicated
   and stressful, so it is important to be able to perform
   well while under pressure. A neurosurgeon should
   also have an uncommon capacity for working long
   hours.

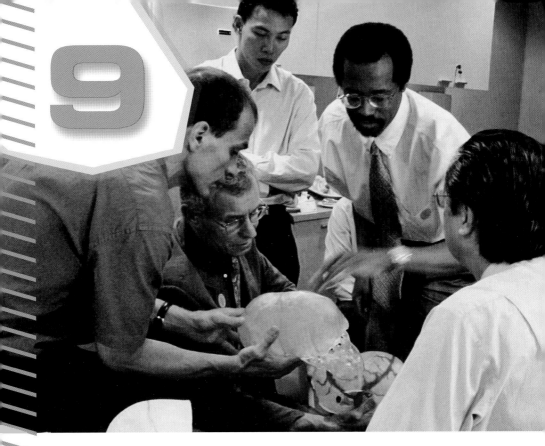

A team of neurosurgeons and medical personnel discuss complicated procedures before operating on the brain.

WOULD YOU MAKE A GOOD NEUROSURGEON?

When you look at the long, hard road to becoming a neurosurgeon, it might seem like the most important qualities you need are incredible desire and dogged persistence. Those qualities are helpful no matter where you go, but the fact is that you don't need to settle on neurosurgery for quite some time. If you complete college and medical school, you have six more years of on-the-job training called a residency. Your first year of residency is designed to give you experience in various branches of medicine, both surgical and nonsurgical.

RISK TAKING AND CONFIDENCE

Surgeons in general have a reputation for being action-oriented, risk-taking individualists. Yet no one in health care depends more strongly on teamwork. Can you be a team player? As a neurosurgeon, some will consider you to be a miracle worker. Still, you will never do it alone. It's important to be able to appreciate the contributions of your teammates.

BEING THE BEST

Do you have a competitive streak? As you move along the path to neurosurgery, competition will be constant for the best grades, the best colleges, the best medical schools, and the best resident programs. You'll also

"The myth of the brain surgeon is largely that—a myth. While one can't be stupid and be a neurosurgeon, brain surgery isn't the most intellectually demanding occupation on earth. I can read a CT scan, but the people who designed and built the scanner's circuits tower over me in cognitive power. I can see a blood clot crushing the life from a brain and deduce that the clot should be removed, but Gomer Pyle would come to the same conclusion."[1]

—*Frank Vertosick, Jr., MD*

be in competition for the best surgical reputation, the best research papers, and the best hospital or university post. If your response is "Bring it on!" then you might enjoy the journey.

ORGANIZATIONAL SKILLS

Are you neat and organized in most areas of your life? Not all neurosurgeons are personally neat, but operations are called "procedures" for a reason. You need to know how to follow surgeries step by step, while noticing if anything is out of place. In addition, organizational skills will be essential on the long educational road to your goal.

"I used to think that the hardest struggle of doctoring is learning the skills. But it is not, although just when you begin to feel confident that you know what you are doing, a failure knocks you down. It is not the strain of the work, either, though sometimes you are worn to your ragged edge. No, the hardest part of being a doctor, I have found, is to know what you have power over and what you don't."[2]

—Atul Gawande, MD

HELPING OTHERS

The most important quality for a neurosurgeon is sometimes overlooked when thinking about the challenges of medical school and training. As in all medical professions, you must sincerely want to help people. At the height of an operation, you may focus on a brain or a spine, but you do that so you can save or improve the life of a person.

So, don't neglect your people skills: compassion, empathy, and communication. Disorders of the brain and nervous system can afflict people in terrible ways, and you will need all three of these skills when speaking with patients and their families.

CHECKLIST

Is neurosurgery right for you? Take a look at this checklist to see if this career is a good fit.

- *Are you interested in math and science, especially chemistry and biology?*

- *Are you eager to help people?*

- *Do you perform well when you have competition?*

- *Can you make quick decisions in an emergency?*

- *Are you detail oriented?*

- *Are you a good listener?*

If you answered yes to the questions above, you already have some of the qualities that make a good neurosurgeon. If you answered no to one or more, don't worry. You can develop all of these traits, even the eagerness to help, if you are willing to make the effort.

HOW TO GET THERE

HIGH SCHOOL

"Recent studies contradict the popular notion that doctors who perform challenging procedures . . . are 'born with good hands,' that they have innate talent in manual dexterity. Of course, if you are a complete klutz, manipulating instruments in a child's heart would not be your ideal career path. But this research on physician performance of procedures shows that 'visual-spatial' ability, meaning the capacity to see in your mind the contours of the blood vessel or the organ, rather than the nimbleness of your fingers, is paramount."[3]

—*Jerome Groopman, MD*

A high school student should take Advanced Placement science and math courses and get great SAT scores, especially in the math portion. English and health courses are also important. You should research colleges and universities with a premedical program. Check out how many graduates of the schools you are considering have been accepted at medical schools.

If you can talk with a neurosurgeon, ask questions about the profession. Read doctors' memoirs, such as *Another Day in the Frontal Lobe: A Brain Surgeon Exposes Life on the Inside*, by Katrina Firlik, or check out blogs by medical students. Medical interns and residents are often eager to share their day-by-day stories. You should also visit the Web sites of professional associations such as the American Medical Association and the American Association of Neurological Surgeons. Immerse yourself as much as you can in the world of doctors and medicine. Try volunteering or job shadowing at a hospital.

In medical school, students study different medical specialties.

NEUROLOGY VS. NEUROSURGERY

What's the difference between a neurosurgeon and a neurologist? While both treat the central nervous system, the neurologist uses medicine and other means rather than surgery. Neurologists treat some problems that a neurosurgeon might not, such as stroke or multiple sclerosis. Both specialties treat some conditions, such as brain tumors, because tumors may or may not require surgery. And neurologists and neurosurgeons often collaborate on the care of a patient. After a neurosurgeon removes a brain tumor, for example, a neurologist may still treat remaining problems with movement or sensation. Neurologists train for ten to 12 years to become certified in their specialty.

COLLEGE AND BEYOND

The standard premedical curriculum at most colleges and universities includes one year of biology, two years of chemistry, one year of physics, and, at some schools, one year of mathematics. To get into medical school you need a 3.5 GPA and you need to have a good Medical College Admission Test (MCAT) score. Once you are admitted to medical school, as one neurosurgeon explains, "You can decide on any medical or surgical specialty. And you rotate through the different specialties and you see what you like or which professor inspires you. But you have to want to work hard because residency is hard."[4]

In your first year of residency, you will continue rotating to different specialties. By the second year, if you choose neurosurgery, you will work as a resident for the next five

Neurosurgery students gain valuable experience and knowledge while in residency at a hospital.

years, progressing from junior to senior resident and, if all goes well, to chief resident in your last year. With each year, you will be given more responsibility, autonomy, and authority over newer residents.

GET YOUR FOOT IN THE DOOR

Fields in medicine are called "helping professions" for a reason. As you explore the fields, you'll find that most medical professionals are happy to answer your questions and introduce you to their work.

Start close to home and work your way out from there. If you are interested in neonatal nursing, think about whom you may be connected with in the field. Do you have any nurses in your family? Are your parents, siblings, or friends involved in nursing? Maybe someone you know has recently had a child and could tell you the name of a nurse who helped her. The same goes for physical therapists—ask around and you'll probably find someone you know who has received physical therapy and could steer you to a professional.

If at first you can't meet with a practitioner of the medical career that interests you, talk with one of their assistants, aides, or technicians. Volunteering in a hospital is a great way for a young person to get to know medical professionals and see what they do. Call a hospital near you and ask about its volunteer program. Do you want to talk to a pharmacist? Pharmacists answer questions all day. Most will be happy to answer your questions.

Another great place to learn about medical professions is by visiting a local college or university that offers education in the areas that interest you. Also, students in professional programs often write blogs or post to departmental bulletin boards. You can learn about the profession and what a student's experience is like. You can also find tips on how to get accepted into schools and learn about time management.

PROFESSIONAL ORGANIZATIONS

Here are some professional organizations that you might want to contact for more information about the jobs in this book.

MEDICAL STUDENT

Health Occupations Students of America
www.hosa.org

PHYSICAL THERAPIST

American Physical Therapy Association
www.apta.org

Section on Women's Health of the American Physical Therapy Association
www.womenshealthapta.org

Sports Physical Therapy Section of the American Physical Therapy Association
www.spts.org

PHARMACIST

American Society of Health-System Pharmacists
www.ashp.org

National Community Pharmacists Association
www.ncpanet.org

National Pharmacists Association
www.npha.com/

NEONATAL NURSE

American Nurses Association
www.nursingworld.org

Association of Women's Health, Obstetric and Neonatal Nurses
www.awhonn.org

National Association of Neonatal Nurses
www.nann.org

NEUROSURGEON

American Association of Neurological Surgeons
www.aans.org/

American College of Surgeons
www.facs.org/

American Medical Association
www.ama-assn.org/

MARKET FACTS

JOB	NUMBER OF JOBS	GROWTH RATE	
Physical Therapist	185,500	*much faster than average*	
Pharmacist	269,900	*faster than average*	
Registered Nurse	2.6 million (Neonatal Nurse: 45,000)*	*much faster than average*	
Physician or Surgeon	661,400 (Neurosurgeon: 5,288)***	*much faster than average*	

*Statistic from the Academy of Neonatal Nurses
** Statistic from DegreeDirectory.org
*** Statistic from AMA's *Physician Characteristics and Distribution in the U.S., 2006 Edition*

ANNUAL MEDIAN WAGE	RELATED JOBS	SKILLS
$72,790	audiologist, chiropractor, occupational therapist, recreational therapist, speech-language pathologist	strong interpersonal and communication skills, compassionate, and a desire to help patients
$106,410	biological scientist, medical scientist, pharmacy technician or aide, physician, surgeon, registered nurse	scientific aptitude, good interpersonal skills, a desire to help others, conscientious, and detail oriented
$62,450 (Neonatal Nurse: $66,698)**	diagnostic medical sonographer, licensed practical or licensed vocational nurse, physician assistant	caring, responsible, detail oriented, able to direct others, emotional stability
$339,738 (Neurosurgeon: $462,000)****	chiropractor, dentist, optometrist, physician assistant, podiatrist, registered nurse, veterinarian	a desire to serve patients, self-motivation, a good bedside manner, emotional stability, the ability to make quick decisions

**** Statistic from Careers in Medicine®, a program of the Association of American Medical Colleges
All other statistics from the Bureau of Labor Statistics Occupational Outlook Handbook, 2010–2011 Edition

GLOSSARY

anatomy

A branch of science concerned with the structure of the human body, its different parts, and how the parts work together.

CAT scan

Computed axial tomography, a series of X-ray views taken from different angles to produce cross-sectional images of the bones and soft tissues inside your body.

epilepsy

A disorder which is characterized by abnormal electric discharges in the brain, resulting in seizures or convulsions.

fetal alcohol syndrome

A birth defect caused by the pregnant mother's consumption of alcohol.

gastrointestinal

An issue relating to the stomach or intestines.

MRI

Magnetic resonance imaging, a technique used in radiology to show the detailed internal structure of the body. It is especially useful in seeing inside the brain, bones, muscles, heart, and circulatory system.

nebulizer

A device that converts a liquid to a fine spray for treating a patient through the airways.

NICU
Neonatal intensive care unit, an area of the hospital where extremely premature or seriously ill newborns are treated and cared for.

outpatient
A patient who visits a hospital for treatment, but does not stay overnight in the hospital.

pneumonia
A lung disease caused by infection and resulting in a fever, chills, cough, and difficulty breathing.

residency
The period of clinical training that follows school. Depending on the career course of the doctor, residency can last from one to eight years.

rounds
A series of regularly scheduled visits made by doctors, nurses, and medical students to patients in a hospital.

vertebra
One of the bony sections that comprise the spinal column.

ADDITIONAL RESOURCES

FURTHER READINGS

Figg, William D., and Cindy H. Chau. *Get Into Pharmacy School: Rx for Success!* New York: Kaplan, 2009. Print.

Firlik, Katrina. *Another Day in the Frontal Lobe.* New York: Random, 2006. Print.

Frederickson, Keville. *Opportunities in Nursing Careers.* New York: McGraw, 2003. Print.

Gable, Fred. *Opportunities in Pharmacy Careers.* New York: McGraw 2003. Print.

Humes, Edward. *Baby ER.* New York: Simon, 2000. Print.

Krumhansl, Bernice R. *Opportunities in Physical Therapy Careers.* New York: McGraw, 2006. Print.

Lais, Toni. *Career Diary of a Physical Therapist.* Washington, DC: Garth Gardner, 2008. Print.

Vertosick, Frank, Jr. *When the Air Hits Your Brain.* New York: Norton, 1996. Print.

WEB LINKS

To learn more about jobs in medicine, visit ABDO Publishing Company online at **www.abdopublishing.com**. Web sites about jobs in medicine are featured on our Book Links page. These links are routinely monitored and updated to provide the most current information available.

SOURCE NOTES

CHAPTER 1. IS A JOB IN MEDICINE FOR YOU?

1. Robert M. Centor. "To Be a Great Physician, You Must Understand the Whole Story." *ncbi.nlm.nih.gov*. MedGenMed. 26 Mar. 2007. Web. 10 Oct. 2010.

2. Allison Van Dusen and Ana Patricia Ferrey. "World's Healthiest Countries." *Forbes.com*. Forbes Mag. 8 Apr. 2008. Web. 10 Oct. 2010.

3. Atul Gawande. *Complications: A Surgeon's Notes on an Imperfect Science*. New York: Metropolitan Books, 2002. Print. 7.

CHAPTER 2. WHAT IS A PHYSICAL THERAPIST?

1. US Bureau of Labor Statistics. "Physical Therapists." *Occupational Outlook Handbook, 2010–11 Edition*. US Bureau of Labor Statistics, 17 Dec. 2009. Web. 8 Oct. 2010.

2. US Bureau of Labor Statistics. "Physical Therapists." *Occupational Outlook Handbook, 2010–11 Edition*. US Bureau of Labor Statistics, 17 Dec. 2009. Web. 8 Oct. 2010.

3. Ibid.

4. Tom W. Smith. "Job Satisfaction in the United States." *NORC/University of Chicago*. 17 Apr. 2007. Web. 10 Oct. 2010.

5. "8 Best Careers for Job Satisfaction." *hr.blr.com*. HR.BLR.com. 6 July 2006. Web. 26 Oct. 2010.

6. Steve Wynia. Personal Interview. 9 Nov. 2010.

7. Ibid.

8. Tom W. Smith. "Job Satisfaction in the United States." *NORC/University of Chicago*. 17 Apr. 2007. Web. 10 Oct. 2010.

CHAPTER 3. WOULD YOU MAKE A GOOD PHYSICAL THERAPIST?

1. Bridget Grace Regan. "Tips on Getting into Physical Therapy School." *Cookies and PT*. 6 Feb. 2010. Web. 10 Oct. 2010.

2. "Why a PT?" *moveforwardpt.com*. Move Forward: Physical Therapy Brings Motion to Life. n.d. Web. 25 Oct. 2010.

CHAPTER 4. WHAT IS A PHARMACIST?

1. "The Pharmacy Profession: Transitioning From Prescription Provider To Health Care Manager." *pharmacist.com*. American Pharmacists Association. n.d. Web. 26 Oct. 2010.

2. US Bureau of Labor Statistics. "Pharmacists." *Occupational Outlook Handbook, 2010–11 Edition*. US Bureau of Labor Statistics, 17 Dec. 2009. Web. 8 Oct. 2010.

3. Manthan D. Janodia "Drug Development Process : A review." *Pharmainfo. net*. Pharmainfo. 25 Dec. 2007. Web. 10 Oct. 2010.

4. US Bureau of Labor Statistics. "Pharmacists." *Occupational Outlook Handbook, 2010–11 Edition*. US Bureau of Labor Statistics, 17 Dec. 2009. Web. 8 Oct. 2010.

5. "Best Jobs in America." *CNNMoney.com*. CNNMoney. Nov. 2009. Web. 10 Oct. 2010.

6. US Bureau of Labor Statistics. "Pharmacists." *Occupational Outlook Handbook, 2010–11 Edition*. US Bureau of Labor Statistics, 17 Dec. 2009. Web. 8 Oct. 2010.

7. Eddie Cash. Personal Interview. 7 July 2010.

8. Ibid.

9. Betsy Towner. "The 50 Most Prescribed Drugs." *newsstand.aarp.com*. AARP Bulletin. Oct. 2009. Web. 10 Oct. 2010.

10. Eddie Cash. Personal Interview. 7 July 2010.

11. Tara Kalwarski, Daphne Mosher, Janet Paskin and Donna Rosato "50 Best Jobs in America." *CNNMoney.com*. CNNMoney. 25 Apr. 2006. Web. 10 Oct. 2010.

CHAPTER 5. WOULD YOU MAKE A GOOD PHARMACIST?

1. Curtis Alexander. "Pharmacist Qualities." *Becoming A Pharmacist Tips*. Becoming A Pharmacist Tips. 24 Aug. 2009. Web. 10 Oct. 2010.

2. Deborah L. Shelton. "Common drugs can mix for dire results." *latimes.com*. Los Angeles Times. 24 Dec. 2008. Web. 10 Oct. 2010.

SOURCE NOTES CONTINUED

CHAPTER 6. WHAT IS A NEONATAL NURSE?

1. Florence Nightingale. "Notes on Nursing." *listentogenius.com*. Listen to Genius! n.d. Web. 10 Oct. 2010.

2. US Bureau of Labor Statistics. "Registered Nurses." *Occupational Outlook Handbook, 2010–11 Edition*. US Bureau of Labor Statistics, 17 Dec. 2009. Web. 10 Oct. 2010.

3. "Neonatal Nurse: Career Summary, Job Outlook, and Education Requirements." *degreedirectory.org*. DegreeDirectory.org. n.d. Web. 24 Oct. 2010.

4. "Nation Gets A "D" As March of Dimes Releases Premature Birth Report Card" *MarchofDimes.com*. March of Dimes. 12 Nov. 2008. Web. 10 Oct. 2010.

5. Elizabeth Lopez. Personal Interview. 14 July 2010.

6. Ibid.

7. Ibid.

8. Ibid.

9. Ibid.

10. Brigit M. Carter. Personal Interview. 15 July 2010.

11. Ibid.

12. Ibid.

13. Ibid.

14. Cynthia Archibald. "Job Satisfaction Among Neonatal Nurses." *Pediatric Nursing* 32.2 2006: 176–162. Print.

CHAPTER 7. WOULD YOU MAKE A GOOD NEONATAL NURSE?

1. Jo Adetunji. "Germany's new wunderkind: the world's smallest baby boy." *guardian.co.uk*. guardian.co.uk. 6 Mar. 2010. Web. 10 Oct. 2010.

2. Allan Hall. "Meet the world's most premature baby boy: The incredible 'Tom Thumb', who at 25 weeks weighed less than a can of Coke." *dailymail.co.uk*. Daily Mail Online. 10 Mar. 2010. Web. 10 Nov. 2010.

3. Nancy Crotti. "All in a Day's Work: Kallie Graham, Senior Staff Neonatal Nurse." *startribune.com*. Star Tribune. 23 Sept. 2009. Web. 10 Oct. 2010.

4. Edward Humes. *Baby ER*. New York: Simon, 2000. Print. 85–86.

CHAPTER 8. WHAT IS A NEUROSURGEON?

1. "AANS National Neurosurgical Procedural Statistics Survey Offers Insight into Practice Management World of Neurosurgeons." *AANS.org.* American Association of Neurological Surgeons. June 2008. Web. 10 Oct. 2010.

2. Ibid.

3. US Bureau of Labor Statistics. "Physicians and Surgeons." *Occupational Outlook Handbook, 2010–11 Edition.* US Bureau of Labor Statistics, 17 Dec. 2009. Web. 10 Oct. 2010.

4. "Physician Jobs Information—Salaries." *studentdoc.com.* studentdoc. n.d. Web. 10 Oct. 2010.

5. Claudio Sanchez. "Cost Of Medical School Rises In Recession." *npr.org.* NPR. 9 Mar. 2010. Web. 10 Oct. 2010.

6. Katrina Firlik. *Another Day in the Frontal Lobe.* New York: Random, 2006. Print. 242.

7. Stephen Boone. Personal Interview. 29 Sept. 2010.

8. Ibid.

9. Ibid.

10. Ibid.

11. Sherwin B. Nuland. *The Soul of Medicine.* New York: Kaplan, 2009. Print. 93.

12. Stephen Boone. Personal Interview. 29 Sept. 2010.

13. J. Paul Leigh, Daniel J. Tancredi, and Richard L. Kravitz. "Physician career satisfaction within specialties." *biomedcentral.com.* BMC Health Services Research. 16 Sept. 2009. Web. 10 Oct. 2010.

CHAPTER 9. WOULD YOU MAKE A GOOD NEUROSURGEON?

1. Frank Vertosick, Jr. *When the Air Hits Your Brain.* New York: Norton, 1996. Print. 13.

2. Atul Gawande. *Better: A Surgeon's Notes on Performance.* New York: Metropolitan, 2007. Print. 154.

3. Jerome Groopman. *How Doctors Think.* Boston: Houghton, 2007. Print. 141–142.

4. "Interview with a Neurosurgeon." *e-shadow.com.* e-shadow. n.d. Web. 10 Oct. 2010.

INDEX

ABOUT THE AUTHOR

Richard Reece is a longtime magazine editor and a writer of both fiction and nonfiction. A native of Kansas City, Missouri, he grew up in Minnesota, where he was a middle school teacher for several years. He currently resides in Raleigh, North Carolina.

PHOTO CREDITS

iStockphoto, cover, 3; Ciseren Korkut/iStockphoto, cover; Graham Bell/Corbis, 6; Kiichiro Sato/AP Images, 8; moodboard/Corbis, 12; Shutterstock Images, 14, 41, 76; Eliza Snow/iStockphoto, 16; M. Ali Khan/Shutterstock Images, 18; Ed Andrieski/AP Images, 23; Angelos Tzortzinis/AFP/Getty Images, 28; Colman Lerner Gerardo/Shutterstock Images, 30; Miguel Villagran/AP Images, 36; Dale Wetzel/AP Images, 38; Bochkarev Photography/Shutterstock Images, 46; Sean Locke/iStockphoto, 50; Rogelio V. Solis/AP Images, 54; Karen Kasmauski/Science Faction/Corbis, 56; Claude Paris/AP Images, 59; Louie Psihoyos/Corbis, 63; Stefan Sauer/Corbis, 68; Daniel Giles/AP Images, 72; Tia Owens-Powers/AP Images, 75; Barry Slaven/Visuals Unlimited/Corbis, 79; Roger Ressmeyer/Corbis, 85; Raffles Hospital/AP Images, 88; Olaru Radian-Alexandru/Shutterstock Images, 93; Ocean/Corbis, 95